FOO FIGHTERS
THE BAND THAT DAVE MADE

Previous: Foo Fighters current line-up. (L-R) Rami Jaffee, Nate Mendel, Taylor Hawkins, Dave Grohl, Chris Shiflett, Pat Smear

This page: Reading Festival, 2005

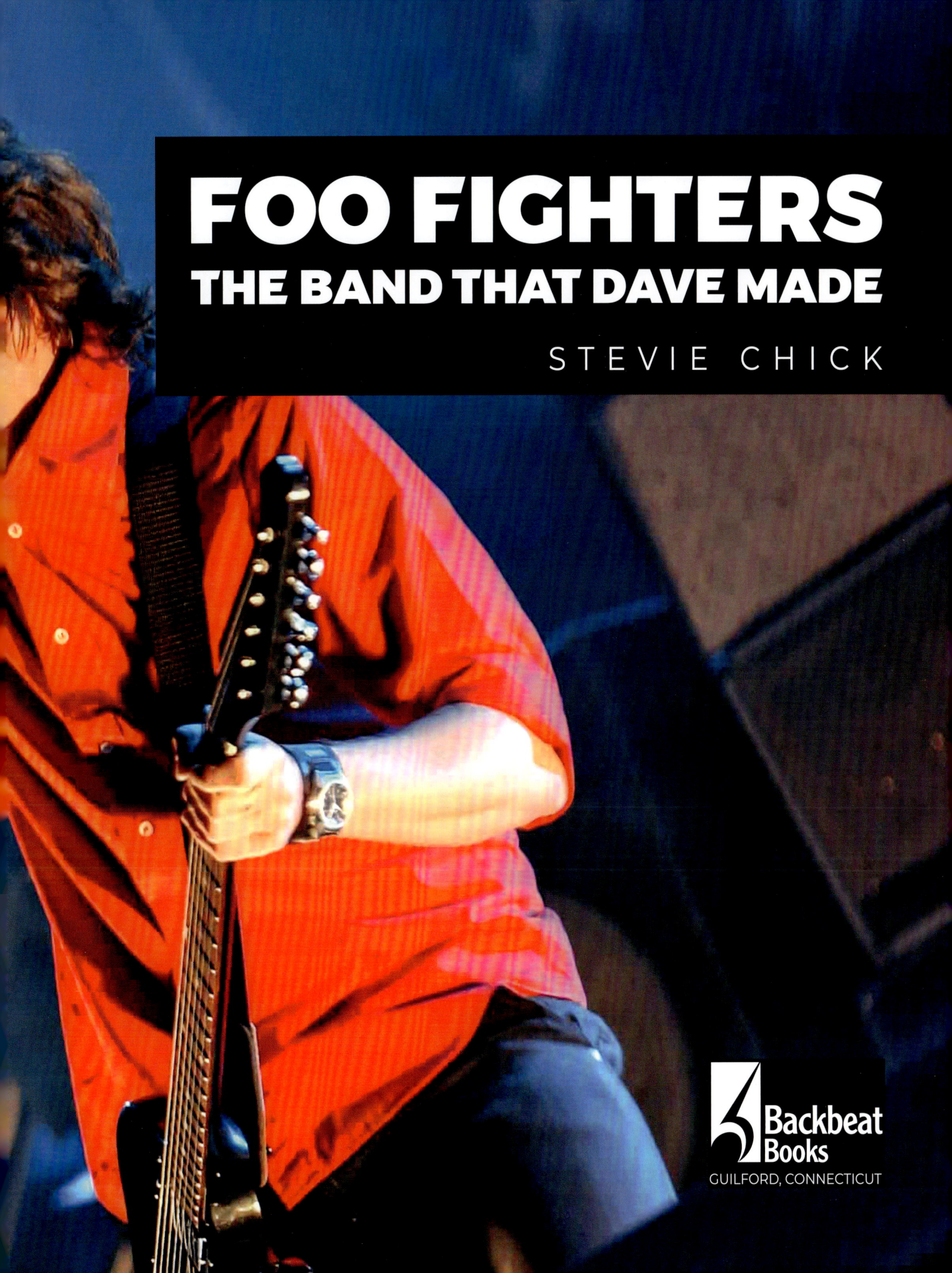

Published by Backbeat Books
An imprint of The Rowman & Littlefield Publishing Group, Inc.
4501 Forbes Blvd., Ste. 200
Lanham, MD 20706
www.rowman.com

Distributed by NATIONAL BOOK NETWORK

Design and layout © 2019 Palazzo Editions Ltd
Text © 2019 by Stevie Chick

Created and produced by
Palazzo Editions Ltd
15 Church Road
London, SW13 9HE
United Kingdom
www.palazzoeditions.com

All rights reserved. No part of this book may be reproduced in any form or by any electronic or mechanical means, including information storage and retrieval systems, without written permission from the publisher, except by a reviewer who may quote passages in a review.

Library of Congress Cataloging-in-Publication Data available

ISBN: 978-1-61713-730-3

∞™ The paper used in this publication meets the minimum requirements of American National Standard for Information Sciences—Permanence of Paper for Printed Library Materials, ANSI/NISO Z39.48-1992

10 9 8 7 6 5 4 3 2 1

Colour reproduction by XY Digital Ltd
Printed and bound in China by C&C Offset Printing

This page: *Live Earth*, July 2007

Contents

I'll Stick Around 6

Alone + Easy Target 22

This Is A Call 38

This Is A Blackout 58

Learn To Fly 74

Times Like These 94

Best Of You 114

Stranger Things Have Happened 136

A Matter Of Time 158

Congregations 180

The Sky Is A Neighborhood 202

For Sarah and Marin, for their infinite patience
and inspiration *and* for Anton Brookes, for all
the Foos times, but especially LA in 2005

I'll Stick Around

"Okay. So. We're the Foo Fighters. Thank you for coming. I'd like to ask you one favor. I know there's a lot of you out there—if you could just. Be. Nice. [laughs] Be nice to each other, it'll be really fun."

— **DAVE GROHL, AUGUST 26, 1995**

Foo Fighters, 1995. (L-R) William Goldsmith, Nate Mendel, Dave Grohl, and Pat Smear

Little John's Farm is an unremarkable stretch of land in the Thames Valley, just south of the river Thames in England. It doesn't boast any ley lines or ancient pagan mythos like the UK's other main festival ground, Glastonbury. But magic still occurs here, every August Bank Holiday, as this humble grassland plays host to rock groups, metal acts, funk arkestras, punk collectives, and miscellaneous vagabond noiseniks from across the world.

For the Reading Festival, 1995 will prove to be a banner year, with Smashing Pumpkins, Björk, and Neil Young headlining across the three nights, along with a coterie of stars and soon-to-be-stars. But the performance the Reading massive is most stoked about is happening far away from the main stage, in a smaller tent sponsored by the now-defunct weekly music magazine *Melody Maker*. The group in question are making only their second appearance on a British stage; their debut album having hit the shelves barely six weeks before. But right now, Reading attendees are so desperate to see Foo Fighters play that they're shimmying up the tent supports and hanging from the rafters.

Dave Grohl's been to Little John's Farm before; twice, in fact. First in 1991, when his previous group were one of a slew of American underground acts invading European festival stages that summer, a canny pre-echo of a cultural zeitgeist-shift that was about to occur. A year later, that group closed the festival on the main stage amid a torrent of insanity, soap opera, and gossip, with an unforgettable performance many believed their frontman would be too insane, too junk-sick, or too dead to play. It would be their final appearance on British soil.

That group was Nirvana, and only a year or so on from their demise—following the tragic suicide of bandleader Kurt Cobain—it's hard to argue that they weren't the defining cultural phenomenon of their generation. Many artists performing at Reading this weekend are inexorably linked to Nirvana, from friends like Mudhoney, to Cobain's nemesis Billy Corgan of Smashing Pumpkins, to Kurt's widow, Courtney Love, and her band Hole. None, however, have the weight of expectation bearing down upon them quite like Nirvana's drummer Dave Grohl, fronting a new band of his own, performing on the site of that group's past (and most poignant) triumphs, and inviting inevitable comparisons with his friend and former bandmate.

But then, along with being the nicest bloke in rock, Dave Grohl is also one of the most perceptive. He knows he'll be enduring those comparisons for the rest of his days. And he also knows that, ultimately, those comparisons don't matter for shit. What matters is what he does with the rest of his life. Starting with right now.

Ten years on from that fateful Reading festival, and I'm sat in the kitchenette of Dave Grohl's plush new recording studio, Studio 606 West, in Northridge, Los Angeles. Grohl has plowed $750,000 of his own money into the studio, which has been designed to painstakingly replicate Polar, the Stockholm recording studio founded by Abba's Björn Ulvaeus and Benny Andersson, where Led Zeppelin recorded their final album, *In Through The Out Door*. The studio is kitted out with the best equipment money can buy, but despite the eye-watering price-tag, still bears the ambiance of a teenaged rock obsessive's clubhouse. The walls are decorated with Gold and Platinum disks for albums Grohl's been involved with; the cushions on the sofas are dressed in pillowcases Grohl's mum has fashioned from his beloved old band tees. "I have a great place to work," grins Dave.

Right now, Dave's recalling the circumstances of his joining Nirvana, perhaps as fateful a juncture as any in his young life. Grohl had been drumming with D.C. hardcore legends Scream, but that band had run aground while touring in Los Angeles, leaving Grohl stranded and living with his guitarist's sister and her two mud-wrestler flatmates at the Hotel Tropicana in Laurel Canyon. Salvation arrived when Grohl's friend Buzz Osborne, of sludgy grunge pioneers the Melvins, called to tell Grohl of a band in the Pacific Northwest who'd been impressed by how hard he'd pounded the skins when Scream had played San Francisco. Said group were looking for a new drummer, and Dave had literally no better options on the table.

"I called them, and we talked about music," Grohl remembers. "Everything from Neil Young to Public Enemy, from Black Flag to Black Sabbath. I bought a copy of their debut album, *Bleach*, played it ten times, then went to U-Haul, bought a big fucking cardboard box, dismantled my drum kit, threw my duffle bag in it, and flew up to Seattle. I showed up there with my big cardboard box, nothing else. Kurt and Krist (Novoselic, bassist) met me at the airport, I recognized them from the sleeve of *Bleach*, they looked like these dirty fuckin' biker children. I didn't expect them to be as sweet as they were. They wouldn't hurt a fuckin' fly."

Grohl spent six weeks crashing at Novoselic's apartment in Tacoma, Washington, before moving in with Cobain in nearby Olympia. "We lived in this tiny apartment that was just an absolute fuckin' dumpster, and I was on a schedule where we would go to sleep about 6.30 in the morning, and

Opposite: Buzz Osborne, lead singer and guitarist of the Melvins, was a key figure in Dave Grohl's joining Nirvana.

wake up maybe around 4.30 in the afternoon, just as the sun was going down. We were doing a lot of rehearsing in this barn out in Tacoma, and we had no television, just a small stack of albums and a 4-track tape recorder, cigarette butts and corn-dog sticks everywhere. My home was the couch, which was about four-and-a-half-feet long, and I'm six-feet tall—it was just a fuckin' nightmare."

It was in Olympia that Grohl and Cobain began to bond. On the surface, they shared much in common, though the devil lay in the detail. Both were children of divorce, Dave's dad, James, leaving the family home when his son was seven, Kurt's parents splitting when he was nine. But while Grohl committed minor acts of rebellion after his parents' divorce—a little occasional vandalism and experimenting with psychedelics—Kurt's parents' divorce had a catastrophic effect upon their son, causing emotional scars that would never heal.

And while music provided sacred succor to both throughout their youth, Kurt's relationship with rock 'n' roll was more complex than that of his new drummer. Grunge—the music scene for which Nirvana would serve as reluctant figureheads—was in many ways the sound of a generation refracting the heavy

Below: Nirvana's 1989 debut album, *Bleach*

I'll Stick Around

Above: The pre-Grohl line-up of Nirvana, circa 1990. (L-R) Chad Channing, Krist Novoselic, Kurt Cobain

Opposite: The bill for the 1991 Reading Festival, with Nirvana low on Friday's main-stage line-up. The following year, they would return as hotly anticipated headliners.

"Kurt and Krist met me at the airport, I recognized them from the sleeve of *Bleach*, they looked like these dirty fuckin' biker children. I didn't expect them to be as sweet as they were. They wouldn't hurt a fuckin' fly."

DAVE GROHL

Left: Grohl's baptism of rock 'n' roll fire: legendary 1980 AC/DC concert movie *Let There Be Rock*

Opposite: H.R. singer with hardcore punk pioneers and Washington, D.C. legends Bad Brains

"My first 'punk rock' experience was going to see the AC/DC concert movie *Let There Be Rock*. That was the first time I felt that energy, like I just wanna fuckin' break something, I'm so excited I might lose my mind. It was dirty, and sweaty, and fuckin' beautiful."

DAVE GROHL

rock they'd grown up with via the punk rock sensibilities they'd subsequently developed. For Kurt, his love of punk rock and his embrace of its politics—not to mention the politics of the super-liberal, "super-woke" college town where he and Grohl were now living—rendered the heavy rock idiom profoundly problematic. These conflicts perhaps explain the fiery potency of Nirvana's fusion of punk rock bristle and metallic volume.

But rock 'n' roll was never problematic for Dave Grohl. His first concert experience was a show by Chicago punk rock quartet Naked Raygun at the Cubby Bear in Chicago, in 1982. "I was thirteen," he remembers. "I loved the intimacy of it. I talked to the singer afterwards, and I jumped on somebody's head, and I felt completely at ease with the band and the audience. It was just a bunch of people having a good time."

But while Grohl fondly remembers catching the face-melting likes of Bad Brains, MDC (Millions of Dead Cops), and Slayer up-close at punk rock DIY events and club shows, that didn't mean he was too cool for heavy rock. "My first 'punk rock' experience was going to see the AC/DC concert movie *Let There Be Rock*," he remembers. "That was the first time I felt that energy, like I just wanna fuckin' break something, I'm so excited I might lose my mind. It was dirty, and sweaty, and fuckin' beautiful."

So Cobain and Grohl made for something of an odd couple in Olympia, and Grohl would later admit he struggled to fit in at parties there, a larger-than-life rock 'n' roll energy force when everyone else wanted to discuss politics and punk. But the pair were forging a deep, profound connection, and Grohl's new friend inspired him to write a song he'd later record for an underground cassette release, *Pocketwatch*, under the pseudonym "Late!" at the height of Nirvana's success—a song he rerecorded some years later for Foo Fighters' 2005 album,

Right: *Nevermind*, Grohl's first album with Nirvana, would make the group an unlikely global phenomenon.

Opposite: Grohl (center) joins the Nirvana line-up, 1990.

In Your Honor. "Friend Of A Friend" was the kind of song you might write late at night, sleeping on a sofa too small for your frame, thinking about this latest twist in a peripatetic life, and trying to capture your new friends in a few lines, a few insightful, haunted observations. It's a song that, even in its simplicity, seems to hint that Grohl senses this friendship might change his life. At the same time, there's a dark undertow to the song, a sense of turbulent forces at work, that not everyone in this story might get a happy ending.

"I wrote the song one night, and recorded it while Kurt was sleeping," Grohl remembers. "I was just writing about these people I'd just met, and writing about myself, too. I had a lot of time to sit around and think."

This period of downtime wouldn't last for long. Grohl joined Nirvana in September, 1990; a year later, the group's breakthrough second album, *Nevermind*, hit the racks, and all hell broke loose. The album turned the mainstream rock paradigm upside down, breaking down the barriers to let a swarming underground rock scene claim the world's airwaves for their own. But its release also set in motion a chain of events that would ultimately result in Cobain taking his own life in April, 1994.

The singer, the songwriter, the blonde, blue-eyed, acid-tongued punk rock rag-doll possessed of *that* firewater scream, with *that* ability to marry melody and misery and malevolence and vulnerability in the same breath—the dazed, fucked-up, tormented kid fronting the band who had come from nowhere to become the biggest thing on the entire planet, at a speed that would have given even punk rock hardman Henry Rollins the emotional bends—Kurt Cobain became the focus of everything Nirvana stirred up in the zeitgeist. The one the media wanted to question and photograph, the one the fans wanted to touch and grab and tear to shreds, the one the industry wanted to run through the mangle and make money off. "And I think some people are built for that, to sustain or survive that, and some people just aren't," Grohl says.

"Each of us processed that experience in different ways," he adds. "My first reaction was, 'Wow, you mean I don't have to go back to work at the furniture warehouse again?' I was fucking relieved that I had finally made some sort of mark with my music. But again, I was the drummer, the one whose face you never saw, my face hidden by long black hair and an enormous 15-inch rack tom. I could walk in the front door of a Nirvana show and never be recognized. So it was kind of ideal for me."

That isn't to say the group's breakneck rise didn't have an effect on the drummer, that there weren't moments when his dream job edged closer to becoming a nightmare. "The thing I started to notice was, people were starting to pull," he says. "People would pull me to an interview, or pull me into the dressing room, and people would push me on-stage. And that's when I thought, 'OK, this is getting a little weird.' There were times where I'd excuse myself from an interview to have a piss, and have an extreme anxiety attack. Like, 'Why am I so stressed, so nervous?' I was pretty overwhelmed. Everything happened over such a short period of time. A lot of it's kind of a blur."

When everything began falling apart, it happened quickly. "By the beginning of 1992, we decided to stop," he remembers. "When *Nevermind* was selling millions of copies, we were basically just hiding from everyone, because we didn't really know how to deal with that kind of success. Once the band blew up, we all spread out a little bit. I went back to Virginia, Krist was up in Seattle, Kurt was over in Los Angeles. Things just

changed. It's no secret that Kurt was battling drug addiction, there was tension within the band over some business matters. It all seems a little clichéd now—you've read that fuckin' biography before—but it actually happened."

They recorded a follow-up to *Nevermind*, *In Utero*, a bloody, beautiful, brilliant, brutal listen. "It was our backlash," Grohl says, "our response to what had happened." It was also, for Cobain, sonic autobiography, a painfully honest piece of work. It was released in a blaze of acclaim and controversy. Cobain, now father to a baby daughter with his wife, Courtney Love, continued to struggle with heroin addiction, and his depression metastasized. While touring *In Utero* in Europe, Cobain overdosed on Rohypnol and champagne: a failed suicide attempt. A month later, following an intervention (attended by Novoselic and Nirvana's touring guitarist Pat Smear, but not Grohl, who was filming a video for a movie soundtrack he'd worked on), Novoselic threatened to break up Nirvana, if Kurt didn't get help. Cobain went on the lam from rehab, got hold of a gun, and took his own life.

Sixteen or so months later, at Little John's Farm, Foo Fighters are playing the most important show so far of their young lives. We'll meet the men sharing the stage with Dave Grohl

I'll Stick Around

Left: Kurt Cobain attends the 10th Annual MTV Video Music Awards accompanied by wife Courtney Love and daughter Frances Bean Cobain.

this evening soon enough, just as we'll trace the route from his darkest moment back towards music, explore the origin story of Foo Fighters' remarkable debut album, and follow the path the group paves from this point onwards.

Right now, let's just concentrate on that hot August night in the Thames Valley, the air thick with heat and sweat, so overpowering that even the Reading Festival's burly security staff are passing out and being carried backstage. Outside wait hundreds of fans, trying to find a way to pack themselves inside the tent, which by now resembles the proverbial sardine can. Inside the tent, they climb the tentpoles and hang from the rigging, and it's all Dave Grohl can do to beg them to stop before they hurt themselves and others, to tell them he won't start playing again until they get down from there.

"If you don't move back we can't play anymore," he says. "Everyone scoot back, like a Fugazi show. I think someone got hurt. I don't want anyone to get hurt, y'know, I just wanna play. You shouldn't either. Because we're all one big family, man. If you see someone who looks like they're passing out, just hold 'em up, don't let 'em get trampled. And don't eat the brown acid, either."

Listening to that Reading 1995 show now, on a ropey, covertly-recorded cassette bootleg, is a revelation. The band had played a slew of shows already that year, including hyped-up industry showcases and a seat-of-their-pants tour supporting hardcore legend Mike Watt across America. But they'd never played a show like this, with so much anticipation, before such an electrified audience, in such challenging conditions. Anyone might understandably crumple under such pressure—especially

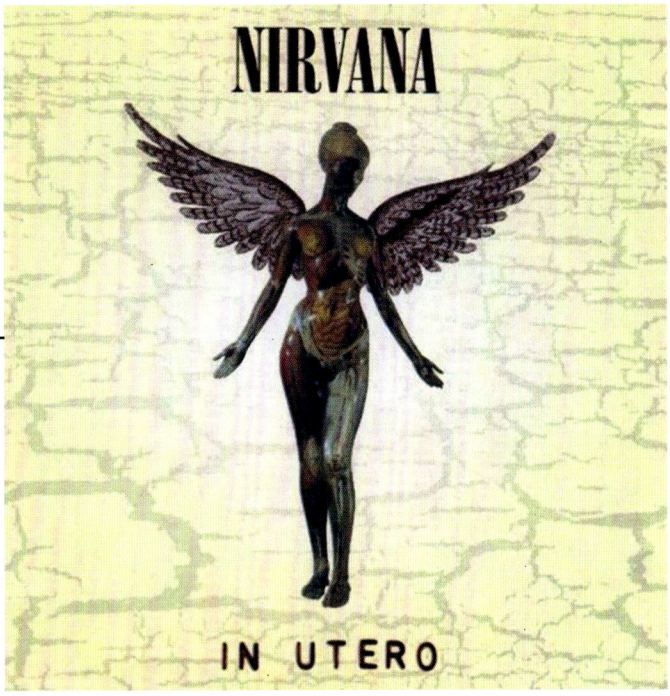

Right: Nirvana's bleak, brutal third album, *In Utero*, captured Cobain's dissatisfaction with stardom. Within a year of its release, he was dead.

Cobain's suicide on April 5, 1994 dominated the rock press for months afterwards.

> "When I worked at Furniture Warehouse playing music was like my vacation. Those weekends meant so much to me. And I still have that feeling."
> **DAVE GROHL**

I'll Stick Around

if they were still reeling from the trauma Grohl had experienced in the preceding months.

The confidence, the easy onstage bonhomie, the ability to joke with a stadium full of fans like they're friends sat in his front room—skills he displays every night he's on the road today—are absent here tonight. They will come to Grohl in good time. There are moments when Grohl seems momentarily cowed by circumstances, when fear of his fans getting hurt almost leads him to cut the show short. But still, instead, he finds that same courage that pushed him out of his bedroom, that dragged him from his slough of despond and put him back onstage, navigates the chords of these protean blasts of anthemic punk rock, and powers through the chaos to the finish line.

The key song tonight—and of the Foo Fighters' eponymous debut, and perhaps of Grohl's entire songbook—arrives five or so minutes into the set, following the opening hurtle of B-side "Winnebago." The song takes all the uncertainty, all the pain, all the fear and all the ugliness of the years before, and purges them in a cathartic chorus scream of "I don't owe you anything!" Dave attacks the song with righteous venom, voice slipping from melodic howl to desperate, Valhalla-I-am-coming scream, like he knows this is his anthem, like this is the story he will make his life: of survival, of thriving, of learning from mistakes, not repeating them. This is the theme of "I'll Stick Around," and it is glorious.

Nirvana crashed and burned, and almost took Grohl with them. The experience took the thing he loved most of all, and almost poisoned it forever. Foo Fighters, then, are an exercise in celebrating that thing he loves. "When I worked at Furniture Warehouse and only played music at weekends," he tells me in 2005, "playing music was like my vacation. Those weekends meant so much to me. And I still have that feeling."

Foo Fighters don't just survive their Reading baptism of fire—the show is a triumph, and a preview of what is to come, for Grohl and for the band. But as the stakes get higher, the times get wilder, and his ambitions grow, those happy endings are by no means guaranteed. It's going to take every ounce of Dave Grohl's energy, talent, blood, sweat, and tears to make this thing happen, and to keep the show on the road.

Left: Grohl finds his joy in music. Seen here pounding the skins as Nirvana record their appearance on MTV *Live and Loud* in Seattle, December, 1993.

Dave Grohl; one of the finest drummers of his generation

Alone + Easy Target

"It was difficult to listen to music, whether it was Ry Cooder's soundtrack to *Paris, Texas*, or Metallica's *Ride the Lightning*. I had to disconnect. And I couldn't imagine getting up there and playing the drums with someone, and not thinking about Nirvana."

DAVE GROHL

It's summer 1994, and Dave Grohl has escape on his mind. Only a few months earlier, ambushed by depression and a debilitating heroin addiction, his friend and bandmate Kurt Cobain killed himself. Scarcely able to process the trauma or the loss, Grohl is struggling to make sense of his life, to locate solid ground, to rediscover some kind of stability. He's a man in search of peace.

Grohl thinks he'll find it three thousand or so miles away in Ireland, where he and new bride, the writer and photographer Jennifer Youngblood—whom he married the month after Cobain's suicide, following a year-long engagement—have gone on honeymoon. Their choice of location is guided by Grohl's love for Ireland, which he first discovered three years earlier, during his first trip to Europe with Nirvana. It was after a particularly lively show at Sir Henry's in Cork, three days after filming the fateful promo video for "Smells Like Teen Spirit," that Grohl sensed the Irish blood that coursed through his veins, giddily calling up his mother, Virginia—maiden name Hanlon—back home, and telling her all the women there looked like her.

In Ireland, Grohl tries to decompress, far away from the tragic soap opera his life has become. Here, maybe, he can escape all the questions about the recent past, and the even more vexatious questions about his present, and his future. He can't even think about music right now, certainly not making it. "If you have someone that's close to you, someone that you love, and they pass away. . .Imagine walking into their bedroom, full of their things, every day," Grohl told me in 2005. "That's exactly how playing music felt to me. It was difficult to listen to music, whether it was Ry Cooder's soundtrack to *Paris, Texas*, or Metallica's *Ride the Lightning*. I had to disconnect. And I couldn't imagine getting up there and playing the drums with someone, and not thinking about Nirvana."

Even here, though, as he and Jennifer drive along the green and pleasant land of Ireland, there is no respite. They spot a young hitch-hiker someway up the tarmac, and make moves to pick him up. A closer look reveals the hitch-hiker is sporting a Nirvana T-shirt. Grohl grimaces, and speeds on.

Hard as he might find it to even think about music, songs still find their way to Grohl. During their honeymoon, in a hotel bathroom, strumming on a mini-electric guitar he'd purchased in Dublin, he comes up with a kinetic fireplug of a melody, and words that conjure a sentiment of thanks, and a redoubling of intent. The song is "This Is A Call," and it is his first step towards the future.

Right: County Cork, Ireland, where Grohl sought solace in the months following Cobain's suicide. Instead of peace, however, he found the inspiration to continue making music.

Right: *2112*, the 1976 landmark album by Rush. The epic work of drummer Neil Peart helped seduce Grohl from guitar and towards the drum stool.

Anyone who'd seen Nirvana play knew that Dave Grohl was a formidable drummer, perhaps the finest of his generation. Back in 1994, however, his skills as a songwriter were known to only the most dedicated of the group's fans.

The drums had been Grohl's first true love, ever since he heard Edgar Winter's bizarro-funk masterpiece "Frankenstein." He went on to spend a childhood summer learning to hammer every beat Neil Peart played on Rush's *2112*, using pillows and his bed as a makeshift drum kit. But he'd also been writing songs since learning how to play guitar in junior high: his maiden voyage on the seas of songcraft, "Bitch," was a heartfelt tribute to the family pooch. Later, he'd help write the songs on Scream's final album, *Fumble* (recorded in 1989, but unreleased until 1993), and released *Pocketwatch* in 1992.

Pocketwatch was culled from two sessions Grohl had recorded with friend Barrett Jones, first while he was drumming with Scream, and then just after he'd joined Nirvana. Grohl handed a cassette of these recordings to Jenny Toomey—frontwoman of indie-rock group Tsunami—who ran her own record label, Simple Machines, from her home in Virginia. She offered to release them on her Tool Cassettes Series, a sub-label within Simple Machines that circulated music via cassette, a format which was cheaper than CD or vinyl. Toomey dubbed cassettes from her home and sold them via mail order. Credited to "Late!," *Pocketwatch* slipped out in 1992 with little to no fanfare, and was mostly overlooked by Nirvana fans until Foo Fighters' later success revealed its existance. Indeed, Toomey struggled to keep up with this belated demand for her home-dubbed cassettes,

> "I felt I had to do it, to exorcise something from my soul. To feel like life keeps moving forward."
> **DAVE GROHL**

while the original master tapes began to disintegrate, forcing Toomey to pull *Pocketwatch* out of print. To this day, Grohl has resisted requests to give it a mainstream release.

Grohl contributed only one song to the Nirvana canon—"Marigold," a track originally from *Pocketwatch* that the band rerecorded during the sessions for their final album, *In Utero*. It was released as the B-side to the single "Heart-Shaped Box"—but Kurt Cobain was an admirer of his drummer's extra-curricular compositions. Grohl later recalled playing Cobain a demo of "Alone + Easy Target" late in 1991. The Nirvana frontman listened to the track on a Walkman while lying in a hotel bathtub. When the tape ended, Grohl told *MOJO*'s Paul Brannigan: "He took the headphones off and kissed me and said, 'Oh, finally, now I don't have to be the only songwriter in the band!' I said 'No, no, no, I think we're doing fine with your songs.'" Cobain also signaled a never-fulfilled interest in recording Grohl's song "Exhausted," though he wanted to rewrite the vocals, which thrilled the drummer: "To have that beautiful voice over one of my songs would have been amazing," Grohl says.

He continued to write music throughout his time with Nirvana, demoing material at home on his 8-track recorder, singing and performing all the parts himself, though modesty and a sense of the enormity of Cobain's talent stopped him from pursuing any serious ambition as Nirvana's secondary songwriter. These humble, homespun songs were written for the same reason he wrote "Bitch" all those years ago: because he could, because it was fun.

Now, in a future without Nirvana stretching before him, writing and recording his own music became less a hobby, and more of a necessity. The man who, weeks before, couldn't even listen to music, now discovered that music might, in fact, prove his salvation. In the copious spare hours he now had at his fingertips, Grohl continued writing new songs, and refining older songs he'd already demoed. "I felt I had to do it, to exorcise something from my soul," Grohl said later. "To feel like life keeps moving forward."

After returning home from his honeymoon, Grohl receives a postcard from the surviving members of Seattle riot grrrl band

Left: Foo Fighters required Grohl to adopt roles unfamiliar to him, becoming singer, songwriter, guitarist and—most challengingly—rock 'n' roll frontman.

7 Year Bitch, whose guitarist Stefanie Sargent died at the age of twenty-four after mixing alcohol and heroin at a party, and whose dear friend Mia Zapata of kindred punks The Gits was raped and murdered the following year. In response to these traumas, the group reunited and cut 1994's ¡Viva Zapata!, a searing album steeped in death, but full of life.

"We know what you are going through," the postcard reads. "The desire for music is gone now, but it will return. Don't worry."

Sure enough, that desire begins to return. Grohl was even feeling strong enough to sit behind the drum kit again. First comes a request from Mike Watt, a veteran of Los Angeles's caustic hardcore scene, a working class hero always sporting a plaid shirt. Watt's first band, Minutemen, split punk rock's atom with wild jazz, fevered punk, and spirited folk, before frontman D. Boon was killed in a road accident in 1985. Watt knows loss, and knows the healing power of music, and the road.

Having won a major-label deal in the wake of grunge, Watt's working on an album, *Ball-Hog or Tugboat?*, with an all-star cast including members of Black Flag, Sonic Youth, Dinosaur Jr., and the Pixies. He invites Grohl to play on the album's opening two-track salvo, laying down drums and lap-steel on "Big Train" and "Against The 70's" where he joins a cast of grunge survivors—including Screaming Trees guitarist Gary Lee Conner, Pearl Jam singer Eddie Vedder, and Nirvana bandmate Krist Novoselic—in a valiant anthem championing punk rock ethics over "stadium minds with stadium lies." "Watt's inspirational, a 'lifer'," Grohl says. "He does it because he loves it, and he'll never stop."

Another lifer enters the fray—Tom Petty, whose Heartbreakers crawled from the south in the early seventies and bested an avaricious turncoat music industry on multiple occasions. The Heartbreakers' long-serving drummer Stan Lynch has just exited the group, and there's an appearance on *Saturday Night Live* on November 19, 1994 hovering on the horizon. "Dave Grohl was our favourite drummer now and he wasn't doing anything, so I called his office," Petty recalled to *MOJO*'s Mat Snow in 2009.

Grohl accepts Petty's offer almost instantly. "I was, like, 'What the fuck? Why's he calling me?' He could get thousands of drummers ten times better than me," Grohl told me in 2005. "I came down to Los Angeles a few weeks later, jammed with them for a weekend, and within two days I felt like a member of that band. They were the sweetest, most welcoming people I'd ever met in my life. And we sounded good. I never asked Tom why he chose me; I think he said something about his teenage daughter being a Nirvana fan and making him do it. That guy's one of America's greatest songwriters." Grohl repairs to the Heartbreakers' practice space and gets to work, learning "Honey Bee" and "You Don't Know How It Feels" from Petty's latest album *Wildflowers*, for what would be Grohl's first TV performance since Kurt's death.

Opposite: Selene Vigil, performing with her band 7 Year Bitch in 1990. A note of encouragement from the band gave Grohl crucial inspiration.

Right: Mike Watt, former bassist with Minutemen and venerated punk rock journeyman, pulled Grohl from the slough of despond, to guest on his solo album.

Left: Rock legend Tom Petty invited Grohl to drum with his Heartbreakers, an offer he was willing to make permanent, had Grohl not wanted to pursue his own music.

Opposite: Thurston Moore and Kim Gordon of Sonic Youth had been key supporters of Nirvana, and Grohl had joined Moore on the soundtrack to 1994 Beatles biopic *Backbeat*.

"He told me he'd just completed an album on which he'd played everything, so the idea of actually being in a band really appealed to him. But I told him that with that going on, he'd be unhappy with us. He's a terrific musician, a very talented guy."

TOM PETTY

His performance was good enough for Petty to offer Grohl the job full-time. "He thought about it, but was torn," Petty says. "He told me he'd just completed an album on which he'd played everything, so the idea of actually being in a band really appealed to him. But I told him that with that going on, he'd be unhappy with us. He would have been happier doing his own thing with this great talent he wasn't using. He's a terrific musician, a very talented guy. He's become his own force of nature."

Petty's offer was golden, and Grohl might have enjoyed life in the ranks of one of rock's most beloved groups, working under the tutelage of a man whose name represented passion, independence, and integrity within a field where those qualities were rare. But Petty realized Grohl's future lay along a different path—one uniquely his own.

It's October 23, 1994, and Grohl and Barrett Jones are leaving the grounds of Robert Lang Studios in Shoreline, Washington. In their possession are a hundred freshly dubbed cassettes, containing rough mixes of fifteen new tracks—twelve slated for a possible album, plus three future B-sides—recorded over the last six days. Copies of the cassette, credited to "Foo Fighters"—old World War Two pilots' slang for UFOs—will soon become objects of fevered desire within the music industry, word spreading as Grohl hands them to friends, to industry movers, to distraught Nirvana fans he meets in the street. Within weeks, major record labels will be throwing cash and promises around, in their desperation to sign the drummer from Nirvana's new band. By the New Year, the album will already be 1995's most hotly anticipated release, seven full months before it hits the shelves. Just your everyday rock 'n' roll success story; it couldn't have gone any better if Grohl had planned it. Which he hadn't.

"The idea wasn't to form a new band and start over," says Dave Grohl, of the sessions that yielded Foo Fighters' debut album. "The idea was to go down to the studio, down the road, and book six days, which was the most time I'd ever spent recording music of my own."

Robert Lang Studios was founded by pinball-loving welder and metal sculptor Robert Lang, who'd given up a career with Boeing in 1972 after friends asked him to record a gig by their band, Cheeseburger Deluxe; it's only a few blocks from the waters of Puget Sound, the Pacific inlet overlooked by Tacoma, Olympia, and Seattle. Boasting two studios, a 48-track desk, and a basketball court, the studio was built by Robert himself, and is a favorite of local talent, from Alice In Chains to Heart to Soundgarden. Nirvana had tracked their final recordings there in January 1994, cutting "You Know You're Right," which remained unreleased until 2002. Grohl had recorded his contributions to Mike Watt's album here only months earlier.

Though a grander proposition than the venues where Grohl had recorded *Pocketwatch*, he'd approached these new sessions with the same method and modus operandi as his home-made demos: recording every instrumental part and vocal himself, save for a guitar part provided by Greg Dulli of Cincinatti's soulful, infernal Afghan Whigs, with Barrett Jones at the controls. Recording began on October 17, 1994, with Grohl the image of focused industry, cutting the tracks in the order they would appear on the eventual album. His work rate was fierce, and he wasted little time; he completed two takes of "This Is A Call" in forty-five minutes. "It became this little game," Dave told *NME*'s Keith Cameron. "I was running from room to room, still sweating and shaking from playing drums, picking up the guitar and putting down a track, doing the bass, maybe doing another guitar part, having a sip of coffee and then going in to do the next song. We were done with the music in the first two days."

The music Grohl cut during these sessions was a blessed fusion of melody and noise: volume, distortion, dynamism, but also tenderness, and unabashed hooks that could tear your heart open. No major departure from the sound that had sent Nirvana multi-platinum, then. But, as Grohl himself pointed out to *Melody Maker*'s Everett True, a longtime Nirvana confidant, he was a child of American hardcore, raised on the coruscating, razor-edged pop of bands like Hüsker Dü, The Replacements, Flipper, and the Pixies. "For me to put out a free-form jazz record to be as far away as possible from Nirvana would be ridiculous," Grohl added.

But while the Nirvana comparison was unavoidable for Dave's new album, the contrasts were worth investigating. For while Foo Fighters ran true to the metallicized pop blueprint *Nevermind* exemplified, Dave's new album lacked a certain nihilistic edge. Not that it didn't have muscle, or blood under its fingernails—check the devil-driven growl of "Good Grief" or "Wattershed's" gonzo, nosebleeding hardcore slam. But that darkness, that desire to burn everything to the ground—even rock itself—which powered Nirvana's most visceral moments, and which critics so often take on face value as an indicator of artistic primacy, was mostly absent here.

Nirvana's bridge-burning *In Utero*, this was not. Not least because, in the songs' loving embrace of that quiet-loud dynamic, and melodies that evoked vulnerability and struggle and triumph, one can hear Grohl as a man who sees music as his salvation, not his curse; this was the kid who was baptized by AC/DC's *Let There Be Rock* exulting in big rock moves his previous band would have striven to undercut, investing the false ending and coda of closer "Exhausted" with the elusive catharsis he had found in committing this music to tape.

One early Foo Fighters review had it that that the album took Nirvana's fabled "Beatles plus Beach Boys plus Black Sabbath" formula, and then removed the Black Sabbath element. Meant as a backhanded compliment—and underselling the album's ability to rock on a most primal level—the comment misses the fact that the Beach Boys recorded music that was every bit as laden as any nightmares the Sabs ever conjured. Similarly, the anthemic, blood-rush rock Grohl had laid down was anchored by an emotional heaviness delivered with a directness that was occasionally startling.

The majority of the songs dated from Grohl's days with Nirvana; only four—"This Is A Call," "I'll Stick Around," "X-Static," and "Wattershed"—were penned after Kurt's suicide. Perhaps sensitive that his words would be picked over by those searching for clues into that group's demise, some of Grohl's lyrics were indecipherable—the Devo-esque stomp of "Weenie Beenie" mashed his vocals through a wall of distortion, while others were purposefully gnomic and nonsensical, like their observations on "This Is A Call" that "Fingernails are pretty, fingernails are good." References to Ritalin and "Minicyn," meanwhile, were inspired by riffling through Jennifer's younger brother T.R. Youngblood's medicine cabinet.

While only a third of the album had been written during the dark days of 1994, it was recorded in the aftermath, and the context of Grohl's recent history lent the whole set a power, a veracity. You can read the desire to recuse himself from the world that fueled Grohl's Irish sojourn between the lines of "Alone + Easy Target's" roaring statement of resilience, even though he'd penned it months before. The album was characterized by irresistible blasts of pop like "Big Me," Dave's unabashedly goofy, romantic love song to Jennifer Youngblood, and the impossibly anthemic "This Is A Call." But it also harbored the noble ache of "X-Static," and the potent gloom powering "Good Grief"—both conjuring an overcast vibe that balanced the other songs' vibrant, kinetic thrills, and that helped make the dreamy, psychedelic strum of "Floaty" feel like such a glorious escape, or the bruised-and-cornered closing epic "Exhausted" such a resonant climax.

Certainly, that song's opening lines: "I'm not around that much right now / Running exhausted and lost," seemed to

---

Opposite: Afghan Whigs frontman Greg Dulli was the only other musician to contribute to Foo Fighters' debut album, lending guitar to "X-Static."

speak to Grohl's mindset much of that awful year. The album found him embattled, licking his wounds, but hopeful. That bruised, defiant tone is best invoked on "I'll Stick Around," perhaps the track with the most naked of lyrics on the record, and the one that would come in for the deepest forensic investigation when these songs finally escaped into the public domain. Lines like "How can it be I'm the only one who sees your rehearsed insanity?," and in particular the howled chorus of "I don't owe you anything" would soon see Grohl at pains to convince interviewers it wasn't aimed at Cobain. His denials that it was inspired by Courtney Love—Cobain's widow, with whom Grohl would maintain a fractious relationship for years to come—were more muted, however.

For all the fractiousness that surrounded its birth, however, the overall vibe of *Foo Fighters*, the album, is one of optimism—of Foo Fighters the band, too, though we'll measure that over the music that follows. That isn't to say the album doesn't graze its fingertips along the same raw, electrified fault lines of emotion that powered Cobain, creatively. But Grohl took his feelings of fear and of anger, and, instead of following them into a self-destructive maelstrom, he wrought them into redemptive rock epics. The songs on *Foo Fighters* transcended their woes, made something anthemic of them. It turned out Grohl was exceedingly good at that. And he was doing it from Foo Fighters' very first album, with a skill that was impressive, and unforced.

Had Grohl followed his first instincts for the recordings, he'd likely never have had to explain his lyrics, as hardly anyone would have gotten a chance to hear them, and fewer still would have been able to trace them back to Grohl. He'd titled the cassettes "Foo Fighters" in a perhaps vain attempt to preserve his anonymity, something precious to this hitherto reluctant rock star.

"I wanted to start my own record label, press up like 2,000 vinyl copies, release the album with no names on it, no photos, just 'Foo Fighters'," Grohl says, in the vein of Police drummer Stewart Copeland's pseudonymous solo album as "Klark Kent." "The intention was to make music, and knowing I was still in the shadow of this thing that was Nirvana, in order for people to be objective, it had to be completely anonymous. That was the original idea, anyway."

But a record like *Foo Fighters* was never going to stay under wraps for long. Eddie Vedder gave the general public their first chance to hear it, playing a song from the demo tape on Self Pollution Radio—a four-and-a-half-hour "pirate" radio show broadcast from Eddie's Seattle home via satellite across the world on January 8, 1995, and featuring live performances from Seattle stalwarts Soundgarden, Mudhoney, and Vedder's own Pearl Jam, along with a spoken-word piece by Krist Novoselic. Foo Fighters had escaped into the world—and that world went wild.

Grohl relinquished his earlier bid for anonymity, and signed with Capitol Records, the major label that had released The

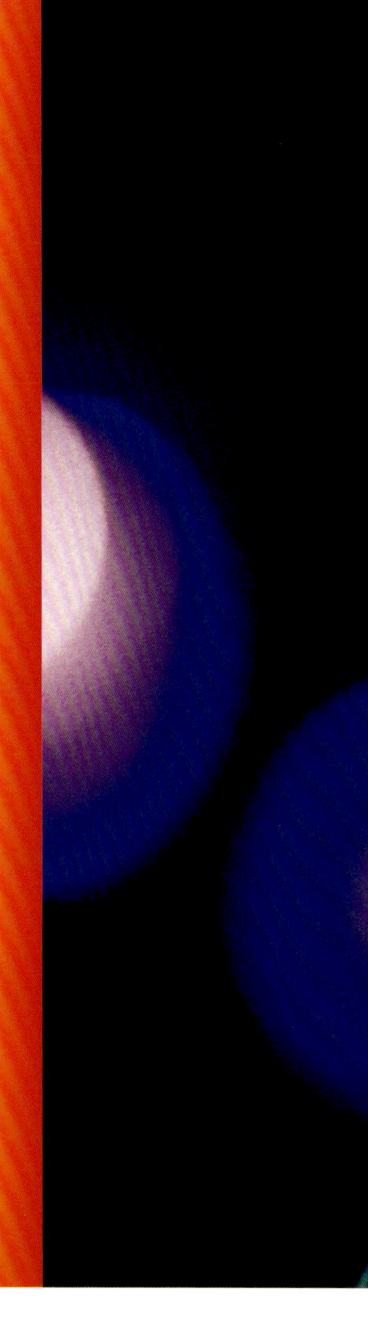

Right: Grohl at Belgium's Pukkelpop Festival, August 25, 1995, one of a series of festival dates Foo Fighters undertook in their first summer together

Beatles' records in the US. Capitol served as parent label to Roswell Records, Grohl's own imprint, which would release Foo Fighters' debut, earning Grohl a higher royalty rate and ownership of his own master tapes. So now the album was going to enjoy a print-run considerably larger than Grohl's initial vision of two thousand vinyl copies, morphing from personal side-project to a major-label release.

But, just as this erstwhile sticksman was reluctant to step from behind the drum kit and take the microphone as frontman, he was doubly reluctant to do so as a lone and easy target. This meant the Foo Fighters would have to become a real, live band.

Alone + Easy Target

"The intention was to make music, and knowing I was still in the shadow of this thing that was Nirvana, in order for people to be objective, it had to be completely anonymous. That was the original idea, anyway."

DAVE GROHL

Foo Fighters: The Band That Dave Made

Alone + Easy Target

Foo Fighters

Released: July 4, 1995
Label: Roswell/Capitol
Recorded: October 14–20, 1994
Robert Lang Studios, Seattle, Washington

PERSONNEL:
Dave Grohl: vocals, all other instruments, production

Additional personnel:
Greg Dulli: guitar on "X-Static"
Barrett Jones: production
Jaq Chartier: jacket artwork
Tim Gabor: art direction, album design
Jennifer Youngblood: cover photo, photography

TRACK LISTING:
All tracks written by Dave Grohl

1. "This Is A Call"
2. "I'll Stick Around"
3. "Big Me"
4. "Alone + Easy Target"
5. "Good Grief"
6. "Floaty"
7. "Weenie Beenie"
8. "Oh, George"
9. "For All The Cows"
10. "X-Static"
11. "Wattershed"
12. "Exhausted"

Left: Pearl Jam frontman Eddie Vedder (right). In 1995 he gave Foo Fighters their first public outing by playing one of their demo songs on his pirate radio show, Self Pollution Radio.

Foo Fighters, August 25, 1995 at Pukkelpop, Belgium

This Is A Call

"When we started this group, I just wanted to make it seem real and in no way contrived. You know, this pretentious sort of, `Rising from the ashes of despair'-type thing. I was like, `Fuck that, man.'"

DAVE GROHL

After their dissolution, bands are invariably asked, "Why did you split up?" But given their natural volatility—thrown together by fate, bound by complex chemistries that scientific genii will never be able to untangle, subject to caprice, whim, and madness, and ever beset by outrageous misfortune—it might be better to ask them, "How did you manage to stay together for so long?"

Dave Grohl entered the process of assembling Foo Fighters with his eyes wide open, freshly familiarized with the combustible nature of the creative unit. Months before Cobain's suicide, unhappiness was already a constant theme within the Nirvana camp. In the final months of his life, Kurt had sought to renegotiate Nirvana's music publishing in his favor, causing tension within his rhythm section, tension exacerbated by the oppressive media interest in Nirvana and their frail frontman, and the increasingly grim tenor of their touring and recording sessions.

Grohl had learned some lessons. He intended to put them into practice.

Most of all, though, he knew he wasn't just looking for sidemen or backing musicians: he was looking for a *band*. "When we started this group, I just wanted to make it seem real and in no way contrived," he told *Q*'s Tom Doyle. "You know, this pretentious sort of, 'Rising from the ashes of despair'-type thing. I was like, 'Fuck that, man.'"

The thing is, "ashes of despair" was a common theme among the musicians who went on to become the first incarnation of the Foo Fighters. All three had, like Grohl, weathered the messy implosions of their earlier bands. The extent to which they were still licking those wounds as they stepped aboard would dictate some of the turns the group's story took in the years that followed.

Formed in 1992, while guitarist Dan Hoerner and bassist Nate Mendel were students and housemates at the University of Washington, Sunny Day Real Estate's music resounded with a subtle, complex, and artfully expressed angst that saw them categorized within the then-nascent "emo" genre. The genre, indeed, was nascent enough that its later evolution into the nervy, multi-platinum pop of Fall Out Boy and their followers was at that time unimaginable. Rather, Sunny Day Real Estate fit in the lineage of bands that fed upon the example set by Rites of Spring. Guy Picciotto's angular, anxious contribution to Washington D.C.'s "Revolution Summer"—that brief era when the region's pioneering hardcore groups disbanded, tired of the violence, the stifling politics, and the sameness that was deadening the region's punk scene—Rites Of Spring existed for only a brief moment, before Picciotto went on to join righteous, politicized, post-hardcore iconoclasts Fugazi. But the influence of Picciotto's songwriting and performances —inverting punk's machismo; foregrounding sensitivity, but never sacrificing one iota of intensity; singing forthrightly, but in his own "more private language"—was potent.

Emo, then, took the dynamics, the volume, the passion of punk, but applied them to personal matters, rather than political causes. Formed from the ruins of an earlier band, Empty Set, which united Hoerner and Mendel with drummer William Goldsmith, Sunny Day Real Estate were rooted in hardcore, but changed direction with the arrival of frontman Jeremy Enigk. An old friend of Goldsmith's, Enigk pulled the group back from the scene's numbskull pelt, investing the gnarly peaks and venomous valleys of their bruised riffage with a roiling, confessional lyrical tumult, as you might expect from a band who titled their debut album *Diary*.

The tempered volatility within the music seemed to seep from the band itself. In an era when the relationship between artist and media was especially tortured, when a band's identity as player of the publicity game was deeply suspect, the group granted a single interview to promote *Diary*, released by Sub Pop in May, 1994, and released a solitary publicity portrait. For all the album's bared-nerve energy, the group themselves aimed to remain anonymous, or at least veiled.

Behind that curtain, however, trouble was brewing. They'd already split up by the time they entered the studio to record their second album in 1995, after Enigk's conversion to Christianity, which followed what Goldsmith later described as two months of seclusion in his bedroom.

Enigk's desire to sing about his newfound faith left Mendel uneasy, while Goldsmith found his bandmate's religious conversion stirred up long-dormant angst relating to the Catholic upbringing he'd since managed to reject. Mendel and Goldsmith later agreed that the band was several miles along the path to oblivion by the time they'd finished touring *Diary*, but Enigk's relationship with Jesus sealed the deal (later accounts attest that, at the close of Sunny Day Real Estate's final show, Enigk began to pray onstage, guaranteeing his estrangement from his former bandmates for a good while).

The unit hung together long enough to complete sessions for their second album, though the band members would later confess that the songs were still in an unfinished state, even as they completed recording them, with lyrics left in sketch form or not even written at all. As if to signify their blasé attitude

Opposite: Fugazi frontman Guy Picciotto, whose earlier band Rites of Spring helped coin the emo genre.

towards this new piece of product, they delivered an album sleeve hardly invested with inspiration—a simple, stark pink cover—and reneged on titling it. Slipping out eponymously, and almost anonymously, the release of *LP2* also marked the breakup of the group.

Though Nate Mendel scarcely realized it, the man who would signal the direction of his post-Sunny Day career was already an element within his social circle; Mendel's girlfriend, after all, was good friends with Jennifer Youngblood. "I first met Dave backstage at a Sunny Day Real Estate gig," Nate told me, in 2006. "Or maybe it was when I went over to his for Thanksgiving once. He was just this genial guy, you know? He went out of his way to make people forget he was in this really huge band. I thought that was really cool, really admirable."

For Grohl, the admiration was mutual. "Nate was very frank, very direct, very polite," he says. "He was a very nice guy." Via Youngblood, Grohl learned that Sunny Day Real Estate was essentially done. Backstage, after what would prove one of the band's final shows, Grohl passed Mendel a copy of the *Foo Fighters* cassette, while Youngblood cannily let slip to Mendel's girlfriend that Grohl was looking for new bandmates. Confluence ruled, and early in 1995, Mendel and Goldsmith were installed as the rhythm section of Foo Fighters. A week or so later, the duo got word from Enigk that he wanted to reform Sunny Day Real Estate and move past their non-musical differences. But he was too late: their connection sealed by a first jam session in the basement of Goldsmith's parents' house, Foo Fighters were about to take flight, with Enigk's former bandmates willful abductees.

There was just one final piece of the puzzle to fall into place, however. The second guitar chair in Foo Fighters would be taken by an old friend of Dave's, who'd accompanied him through Nirvana's darkest days—and was probably hoping lightning wouldn't strike twice.

How punk rock is Pat Smear? So punk rock that when producers of turn-of-the-eighties cop procedurals needed an extra whose mere appearance could sum up the essence of a snotty ne'er-do-well, Pat was the man they asked for. The money from his legendary appearances on TV shows like *Quincy* and *CHiPs* paid the rent in a way actual punk rock scarcely managed to, though there was perhaps never a way a group as debauched, as chaotic, as inchoate as Smear's Germs were ever going to enjoy crossover success.

Self-destructive pioneers of Los Angeles's fast-moving, hedonistic late-seventies punk rock scene, the Germs was fronted by Jan Paul Beahm, who later renamed himself Bobby Pyn before finally being best known as Darby Crash—who memorably appeared struggling to make breakfast in Penelope Spheeris's cinematic document of the era, *The Decline of Western Civilization*. Crash would be dead of an intentional heroin overdose before the movie hit screens in 1980, leaving

Opposite: Sunny Day Real Estate, 1994. (L-R) Nate Mendel, William Goldsmith, and Jeremy Enigk. Mendel and Goldsmith would soon become Foo Fighters.

behind him a sole studio album—the acrid *(GI)*, now rightfully revered as a landmark within Californian hardcore punk—and a sordid life story best retold in the pages of Brendan Mullen's hair-raising biography, *Lexicon Devil: The Fast Times and Short Life of Darby Crash and the Germs*.

In the aftermath, Smear went on to form 45 Grave with fellow Germs survivor Don Bolles, but that group folded after one seven-inch single. By the early nineties, Smear was working at the SST store, the merchandise and record outlet run by the legendary Californian punk rock imprint. But his days as a shop assistant were numbered.

In the months after *Nevermind* broke, the members of Nirvana brainstormed over ways they could ease some of the burdens resting upon Kurt Cobain. One solution lay in hiring a second guitarist to pick up some of the slack onstage, and make touring less of an inexorable grind for Cobain. Dave and Krist imagined Cobain would tap the services of one of their many friends within the grunge inner circle—Steve Turner of Mudhoney, perhaps, or Melvins frontman Buzz Osborne, or Eugene Kelly of Eugenius, whose previous band, filthy Scots whimsicalists The Vaselines, were one of Kurt's favorites. Then Cobain arrived at rehearsal one day and informed his bandmates that Nirvana's new guitarist would be Pat Smear of the Germs. "Krist and I had never met him," remembered Grohl, later. "I just imagined this bloated, tattooed, bitter old mess."

Svelte, bearing no visible tattoos, and certainly by no means bitter, Smear was an instant fit with Nirvana. "Musically, he made the band sound bigger onstage," Krist told me in 2014. But Smear's sonic contribution was secondary to the levity he brought to an often darkening group. Grohl has said that, while legend has it that Nirvana forever traveled under a black cloud, his memories are of fun times on the road, alongside the drama, blowing off steam with post-gig Freddie Mercury karaoke contests. Smear leavened Nirvana's internal chemistry, when they needed it most. "If there were tensions at any time, there was this new guy here," Krist continues, "and he defused things. Pat was so easy-going, so he helped keep things easy-going."

In the months after Cobain's suicide, Smear had secluded himself away in his LA apartment, chain-smoking and living the

"I first met Dave backstage at a Sunny Day Real Estate gig. Or maybe it was when I went over to his for Thanksgiving once. He was just this genial guy, you know? He went out of his way to make people forget he was in this really huge band. I thought that was really cool, really admirable."

NATE MENDEL

Foo Fighters: The Band That Dave Made

Right: Before Pat Smear's arrival, Grohl had imagined that Kurt had lined up Mudhoney's Steve Turner to sign on as Nirvana's second guitarist.

Left: Kurt Cobain (left) performing at the 1991 Reading Festival with friend Eugene Kelly (right) of The Vaselines

life of a bruised couch potato, trying to figure out if there was something he could do next that wouldn't seem like a cosmic anticlimax after Nirvana. It was exactly the sort of question fate takes pleasure in answering.

Shortly after acquiring the Sunny Day Real Estate rhythm section, Grohl dropped by his old bandmate while passing through LA, pressing a copy of the *Foo Fighters* cassette in his paw, but not daring to hope Smear would want to join his new group. But he did, and—after giving him a week to see if he'd change his mind—Grohl welcomed his friend aboard, sensing that Smear's steadying presence would be invaluable as he navigated the choppy waters as a bandleader in his own right, as well as realizing how much he'd missed Smear's wicked grin and his way around a guitar.

> "Krist and I had never met him [Pat Smear]. I just imagined this bloated, tattooed, bitter old mess."
> **DAVE GROHL**

Smear (right) had begun his career playing with seminal LA punk band the Germs, here playing their farewell show at The Starwood, 1980.

Foo Fighters: The Band That Dave Made

Left Grohl, seen here in 1993, would wear the same beloved Michael Jackson T-shirt for his first ever Foo Fighters gig.

Mendel and Goldsmith, however, were initially reluctant to welcome a new addition to their freshly minted ranks, perhaps intimidated by the rapport Smear already had with Grohl, perhaps still adjusting to being in a group that wasn't formed by friends who shared a deep connection, as had been their experience before Foo Fighters. There were still many adjustments for the duo to make, as they graduated from cultdom to what promised to be an altogether wider level of the music industry. Having only toured sparingly with Sunny Day Real Estate, they'd soon find themselves on a grinding, constant performance circuit, in full gaze of a media obsessed with what this Nirvana survivor was going to do next. If they had any anxieties over the new page they'd now turned in their lives, this was probably when those anxieties spoke loudest.

All it took, though, was a first rehearsal for bonds to begin swiftly forming between Pat and Nate and William. No longer merely a Dave Grohl solo project, Foo Fighters were a real, live band. Now all they needed was a gig.

It's hard to properly express just how fierce the anticipation was for the Foo Fighters in February, 1995. It was a time before the Internet as we now know it, and those few souls who possessed original copies of Dave's cassette and wanted to share it with the world could only really do so the old-fashioned way, by dubbing copies off for their mates. Meanwhile, beyond the membranous bubble of the lucky hundreds who'd got their hands on the cassette, rock fans were stirring themselves into a desperate frenzy over just when they might get to see and hear this new band from "the drummer who had been in Nirvana." Foo Fighters' debut album wouldn't hit stores for another five months, and they were already the biggest story in rock music for that year.

> "We wanted everyone to get drunk and be like, 'You guys are really good.'"
>
> **DAVE GROHL**

So, imagine how it must have felt to have found yourself at a cosily grubby kegger above the warehouse of a Seattle branch of West Marine Boating Supplies, just off Mercer Street, on February 19, 1995, to discover that the entertainment that night—setting up their gear on the floor, no fancy stage here—were none other than the Foo Fighters: the band the whole world is desperate to see. The Foos had thrown the party themselves, inviting fifty or so close friends and family to witness the group's first-ever live concert. Grohl even provided the keg, telling *Alternative Press*'s David Daley, "We wanted everyone to get drunk and be like, 'You guys are really good.'"

Cramped into one corner of the stark white space with all their gear, the Foos rocked hard, Dave sporting a sly Michael Jackson T-shirt which he'd also worn at Nirvana's *Pier 93* concert in Seattle, filmed for MTV's *Live & Loud*, in December 1993. It depicted "The King Of Pop," whose *Dangerous* album Nirvana's *Nevermind* had deposed from the top of the charts in January 1992, with a caption beneath reading, "I (heart logo) kids." (Perhaps it was his lucky shirt? Kurt had also been photographed wearing it.) "Afterwards we thought, 'We did it, we pulled it off'," remembered Grohl. "Fifteen minutes after that show was over, Pat and I grabbed each other and said, 'Let's go play somewhere else now.'"

Four nights later, while overseeing final mixes of the album in Los Angeles, the group snuck out to Arcata, a sleepy college town in Northern California, population circa seventeen thousand, for what would be their second-ever gig. While their first had been strictly invite-only, this second show was general admission, though the Foos were performing unannounced, and entirely unplanned. The group had called up Arcata's local rock club Jambalaya the day before and asked if they could jump onto the following night's bill, playing support to covers band The Unseen, whose set list would feature a clutch of Beatles and Elvis Costello favorites..

By showtime on the evening of the twenty-third, word of the Foos' sneak attack on Arcata had slipped out to local rock fans, who descended upon Jambalaya in hordes, quickly overwhelming the venue's strict 220-capacity limit. By the time Foo Fighters hit the stage, nearby G Street had been closed off by the cops, while kids who'd been unable to get tickets pressed their faces against every spare inch of Jambalaya's six-foot-tall windows, desperate to catch a glimpse of these future heroes. Whichever side of those windows they found themselves, the rock fans of Arcata would all agree it was a legendary night.

Afterwards, Grohl manned a makeshift merch-stand, selling T-shirts the band had stenciled in the van on the way over, at three dollars a pop. Nirvana's success had caused a rupture in traditional concepts of punk rock ethics, as underground acts struggled to prosper in an overground

Opposite: Grohl enjoys a warm welcome at The Fillmore in San Francisco on July 26, 1995, on the Foo Fighters' first headlining tour of the United States.

Left: A live album would later be culled from performances on Mike Watt's 1995 *Ring Spiel* tour.

"Fifteen minutes after that show was over, Pat and I grabbed each other and said, 'Let's go play somewhere else now.'"

DAVE GROHL ON FOO FIGHTERS' FIRST GIG

world without "selling out." At Foo Fighters' first public concert, Grohl signaled he was willing to join the melee again, to take his music to the people, but this time it would be on his terms, at a speed he could handle, and a scale he could be comfortable with. He would approach the group's first national tour with a similar mindset.

Following those first two lightning-strike performances, Foo Fighters played a further handful of low-key shows through March, playing rooms like Spaceland in Silver Lake, California; Satyricon in Portland, Oregon (a benefit to help fund a private investigator to solve the murder of Mia Zapata); and the Dingo Bar in Albuquerque. Their first "hometown" show was at the performance space Velvet Elvis on March 4, where Krist Novoselic watched on from the audience as Grohl sang himself hoarse, guided a feral, blitzing "Watershed" towards oblivion ("I've got to get another guitar!" he yelled, at its destructive climax), and wrung every drop of catharsis out of "Exhausted's" aching coda. These staccato baptisms of fire proved the fledgling Foos well up to the task of taking their music to people. It was time to hit the road.

It's around this point that the sturdy road-warrior from the hardcore era, Mike Watt, re-enters our story. His *Ball-Hog or Tugboat?* album hit record shelves in February, 1995 and, as Watt told the *New York Observer*'s Brad Cohan, Grohl and his *Ball-Hog* co-star, Eddie Vedder, approached Watt with a scheme to promote its release. "They came out with this balls-out plan: 'Hey. We'll have our bands open up, and we'll be in your band. We'll come over, we'll have a couple of days practice, and we'll do this.'"

For a man gingerly exploring the world of professional rock 'n' roll one step at a time, taking the Foos on the road with Watt made perfect sense for Grohl: playing modest venues, and only as a support act, suggested the "Ring Spiel Tour," as it would be dubbed, was his way of putting Foo Fighters in "soft open" as a touring enterprise. Similarly, the tour offered Vedder a chance to make music with friends away from the microscope his multi-platinum Pearl Jam were regularly placed under (Vedder would open the shows playing drums with his then-wife, Beth Liebling's avant-garde group Hovercraft).

Left: Grohl and Smear onstage in San Francisco, California, 1995. Grohl found an irreplaceable foil in Smear-though his tenure with the group wouldn't be uninterrupted.

Right: Foo Fighters, backstage at The Tibetan Freedom Concert at San Francisco's Golden Gate Park in 1996.

On the backs of the T-shirts the Foos had printed up to sell on the tour—the first merch they hadn't knocked up in the van themselves—was a slogan reading "The Not Too Terribly Hard Twenty Nine Shows in Forty Two Days North American Tour with Watt." The "Ring Spiel" jaunt kicked off on April 12 at Gibson's, a club in Tempe, Arizona, and continued until May 20, terminating at San Diego State University's Montezuma Hall, with the bands playing to audiences of between three and six hundred each night, for $500 between each band. The plan was, as Watt put it, to "Jam Econo," his unique spiel for touring, and a reference both to the Ford Econoline van beloved of touring bands of a certain budget, and the typical punk rocker's need to keep that budget as low as possible. Sure, there'd be at least a couple of grunge-era superstars on that stage every night, but there certainly wasn't anyone acting like it.

The concerts opened with Hovercraft playing a set of uncompromising space-rock—like *Meddle*-era Pink Floyd, only scarier—illuminated solely by the monochrome flicker of the vintage nature documentaries and outer-space footage projected behind them. Following such experimental, egghead fare, Foo Fighters' thirty-five-minute set was something reassuringly more visceral, more melodic. The quartet typically opened with "Winnebago," a herky-jerky, kinetic blast of hardcore originally cut on *Pocketwatch*, and hurtled through the highlights from their still-unreleased debut album, before closing with "Exhausted," drawing out its climactic crescendos and false endings a little further every night, feeling their confidence grow, and pushing their new audiences further every time. Then, Watt would step onstage and, with Vedder and Pat Smear flanking him on guitar, and Grohl smashing the shit out of his drum kit (occasionally joined by Goldsmith on second drum kit), revisit numbers from *Ball-Hog*, nuggets from Watt's old bands and, on occasion, the odd Blue Öyster Cult, Madonna, or Daniel Johnston cover.

At eight to ten dollars a ticket, attendees got a lot of bang for their buck. The Foos, meanwhile, worked hard, and traveled hard. There were no roadies, no egos, just three vans; one for Watt, one for Hovercraft, one for the Foos—a red Dodge Ram the group dubbed "Big Red Delicious," which Grohl still owns—babbling to each other over CB radio, making up their own trucker lingo and navigating what Grohl later described to *MOJO*'s Roy Wilkinson as "the most exhausting touring itinerary I'd ever seen. That was the beginning of the Foo Fighters, and we have never since toured as hard. That was the perfect way to start—we came off that tour with our teeth cut into fucking razors."

They barely paused for breath, before setting off again. Early June saw the group fly over to the UK, for a legendarily sweat-soaked performance at King's College London, and a show at the Manchester Academy. Then, in July, they set off for their first headlining tour of the US just as the album hit store shelves, playing twenty-six dates throughout the rest of the summer, with Wool, a post-hardcore group featuring Dave's old Scream

bandmates Pete and Franz Stahl, and artful emo group Shudder to Think playing support.

The shows were raucous affairs. Mindful that excitable fans had been getting injured when they attempted to vault across the barriers onto the stage on the first few dates of the tour, Grohl had the barriers removed for the July 27 show at LA's The Roxy. As a result, there were fewer injuries, but the group spent most of the show fielding sweaty, stage-diving fans. That was still preferable to the previous night at The Fillmore in San Francisco, where a misguided attempt to feed the youthful audience some goodness by handing them pieces of fruit as they walked through the door resulted in the band being pelted with apples, oranges, and bananas as soon as they walked onstage. Meanwhile, at the Ogden Theatre in Denver, Colorado, on August 2, one lucky would-be stage-diver was handed Pat Smear's guitar and, after a little low-key jamming, found himself scooped up in a bear-hug by Grohl, before finally leaping back into the maw of the crowd.

It would be fair to say there was a high pitch of euphoria to the Foo Fighters touring experience at this point. They followed the American tour with a blitz across Europe, taking in a number of big festivals (including their tent-busting appearance at Reading) and legendary venues like the Bataclan, before a handful of US shows in September, a full European tour through October and November, and shows in Japan and

Australia at the end of the year. The sheer thrill of being on the road, of playing with this band, had shaken Grohl from his resolution that they would tour only sparingly. Ultimately, they would play 126 shows in 1995.

But while he was happy to spend the lion's share of the year entertaining his fans onstage, Grohl was still only cautiously dipping his toe into the media scrum. Reluctant to subject Foo Fighters to the kind of heavy rotation madness Nirvana had endured, Grohl vetoed filming a promo video for the group's debut single "This Is A Call," while "I'll Stick Around" came accompanied with an off-beat, low-budget clip shot by Devo's Jerry Casale featuring the group rocking out in a room lined with crumpled paper, blitzed by multicolored strobe lights, while a grisly creature hovered about them. In other scenes, Grohl chewed chess pieces and brushed his teeth with Foos-brand toothpaste. It was hardly Tawny Kitaen writhing on the bonnet of a sports car, though MTV did play the clip, to the delight of its dopey animated stars Beavis and Butt-head.

Similarly, the group chose sparing but effective television appearances—making their network debut with a spirited frug through "This Is A Call" on the *Late Show with David Letterman* on August 14 (the first of their eleven spots on the show), and powering through no-frills takes of "I'll Stick Around" and "For All The Cows" for *Saturday Night Live* in December—and were careful to book only a handful of big interviews with the press. Grohl knew that entering this arena would involve fielding a barrage of unwelcome questions over the last days of Nirvana and the death of Cobain, neither of which he was ready to discuss in any depth. What interviews Grohl did grant were mostly with trusted journalists he knew from the Nirvana days, like *NME*'s Keith Cameron and *Melody Maker*'s Everett True.

In the company of these old friends, Grohl was able to let down his barriers, and talk about his recent past, and his brightening future. "Maybe I'm so naive and stupid and childish to think, 'Duh, life must go on,'" he told True. "But if that's what gets me by, then . . . shit. I'll take it. I'm the least charismatic member of the band. A lot of the time, I'm scared to be too emotional, for fear that I'm setting myself up to be shot down. There are a few people that I'll share everything with, but it's like, 'The fuck I'm going to spill my guts out to six million people.'"

As far as what bearing his experiences in Nirvana had upon life within Foo Fighters, Grohl told Keith Cameron that it was very much a question of learning from mistakes. "We all come from these checkered, bruised musical situations," he said, of his new band. "We talked about that when we first got together, about how we didn't want any secrets, any skeletons, to bring everything out in the open so there wouldn't be any problems in the future. And we've been together every day for nearly six months, and it just seems to be getting better and better."

For Grohl, 1995 closed out with an exultant performance at the Summersault festival in North Ryde, Australia—which he opened with a new song, "Enough Space," penned explicitly to open gigs, and drawing its tempo from the excited bounce of UK fans at Foo Fighters shows—and a chance to reflect on how much brighter the future seemed than a year before.

Indeed, things seemed so rosy that Grohl could scarcely have imagined that, within the next couple of years, almost every single member of his band would either have been sacked or have tendered their resignation.

Opposite: The Foo Fighters made it to the cover of *Rolling Stone* magazine in 1995.

> "We all come from these checkered, bruised musical situations. We talked about how we didn't want any secrets, any skeletons, to bring everything out in the open so there wouldn't be any problems in the future. And we've been together every day for nearly six months, and it just seems to be getting better and better."
>
> **DAVE GROHL**

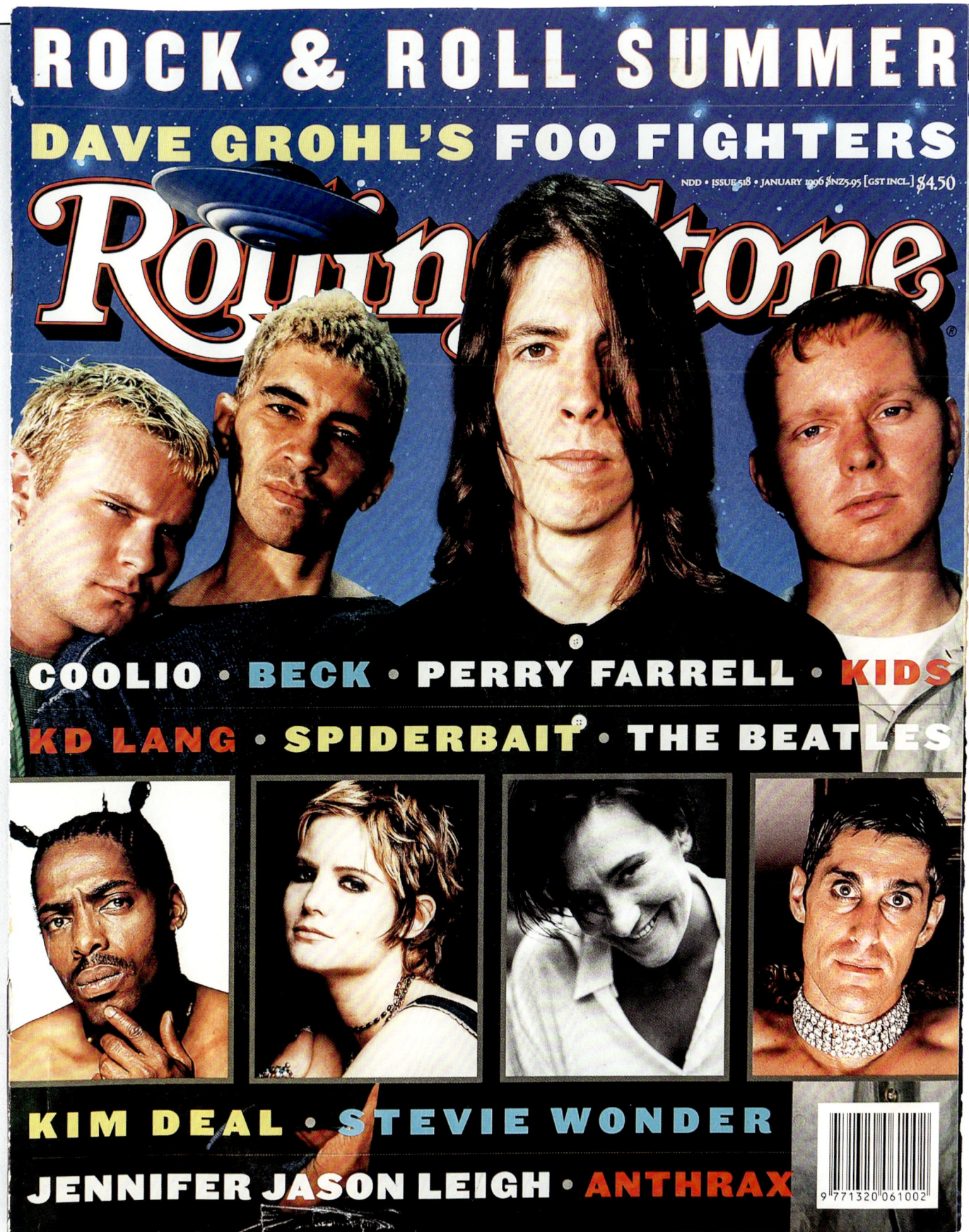

Dave Grohl, London, 1997

This Is A Blackout

"People come up to me, men usually, and say, 'Man, that album helped me through my divorce.'" I'm like, 'Really? It caused mine.'"

DAVE GROHL

Foo Fighters: The Band That Dave Made

A year and a half on from the lowest point of his life, Dave Grohl seemed to have it made. His new band, his Foo Fighters, had quickly become tight friends, and one of the world's most sought-after live attractions. Their debut album, which he'd recorded on his own, in a week, was a critical success and a commercial triumph, selling over forty thousand copies in the week of its release in the US alone, debuting at number twenty-four in the *Billboard* album charts, and going platinum by January of the following year.

He'd even relented on his reluctance towards making music videos, enlisting Jesse Peretz—formerly a member of Boston indie-rockers The Lemonheads—to film a witty promo for "Big Me," a three-minute lampoon of cheesy candy commercials, in which miraculous things happen as a result of people chewing a Mentos-like candy called "Footos." The video was so popular on MTV that, for months afterward, the band would find themselves pelted with Mentos by fans in tribute, and when the group collected the MTV Music Award for Best Group Video for "Big Me" in September 1996, Grohl took the opportunity to announce from the podium that he "would like to think of this award as some kind of closure," imploring MTV viewers to "stop throwing Mentos."

The odd candy-related assault notwithstanding, from the exterior things seemed to be going well for Dave Grohl: he was married, his band was popular, and no critic had a bad word for the group's Grammy-nominated debut album. And though the Foos ultimately missed out on the Best Alternative Music Album award—they lost to Nirvana's posthumously-released *MTV Unplugged In New York*, meaning Grohl was still a winner—life was peachy. What could possibly go wrong?

Well, how about everything?

To celebrate the tenth anniversary of its original 1997 release, Roswell Records prepared a deluxe reissue of the second Foo Fighters album, *The Colour and the Shape*. Along with a clutch of cover versions and B-sides added to the track-listing by way of a bonus, this 2007 repackaging included insightful sleeve notes from Nate Mendel, reflecting upon the album and its somewhat torturous gestation.

"The album was lived in," Mendel began. "In trying to understand the endurance of this record, one needs to look at the circumstances of the recording, and how they shaped the sound. While recording this record, marriages fell apart, we lost a drummer, and we discovered late in the day that record-making is hellishly expensive and best done with a budget prepared beforehand."

And while that short paragraph could be accused of containing spoilers, it does pretty well spell out the story we are about to tell. Indeed, Grohl himself put it pithier, while promoting the album back in 1997, reflecting upon the stressful

Right: The group attend the 1996 MTV Video Music Awards—but not everyone's smiling.

sessions and the complex mood within the band while talking to *Filter* magazine: "I was really proud we actually went in and made a record. And then everyone fucking quit."

For many, *The Colour and the Shape* remains the greatest of the Foo Fighters' albums. It's their best-seller, its success with fans owing much to its emotional content, with Grohl uncorking the great woe within his heart, wishing to be understood about what he was going through during the album's gestation. And it wasn't that gestation itself—legendarily troubled though it was—that was the source of the woes that fuel the album. "People come up to me, men usually, and say, 'Man, that album helped me through my divorce,'" Grohl later told *Classic Rock*. "I'm like, 'Really? It caused mine.'"

The group had finally come off the road following an appearance in the UK at the Phoenix Festival, at Long Marston Airfield, Stratford-upon-Avon. An upstart gathering founded in 1993 as a rival to established annual events like Glastonbury and the Reading Festival, the 1996 Phoenix Festival, which took place from the eighteenth to the twenty-first of July, saw Foo Fighters fourth on the bill of the main stage on the Friday night, performing before Manic Street Preachers, Alanis Morissette, and Neil Young and his Crazy Horse. The show took place around eleven months after the group's triumphant, chaotic tent show at the 1995 Reading Festival, and fifteen months after their first-ever shows together, a period which had mostly been spent on the road—a fact not lost on the members of Foo Fighters who'd joined the group on the understanding that their touring workload would be nowhere near so heavy.

In recent months, the Foos had undertaken another US tour, and appeared at the Tibetan Freedom Concert, an all-star benefit show in San Francisco's Golden Gate Park organized by the Beastie Boys in aid of their Milarepa fund, a charity supporting Tibetan exiles from China and promoting Tibet's independence from China. Before an audience of 100,000, the Foos had appeared alongside Smashing Pumpkins, Sonic Youth, A Tribe Called Quest, Beck, Rage Against The Machine and many more. The Phoenix Festival appearance, meanwhile, signaled the end of another European jaunt booked to follow the American tour, and also the end of promotional duties for the Foo Fighters album.

Perhaps imagining another memorable night like the previous year's Reading Festival appearance, the show was planned to end this intense period on the road on a triumphant note.

However, as *Metal Hammer*'s James Sherry noted in a later interview with Grohl, "At the end of 18 months touring their debut album, the band played at the Phoenix Festival and gave considerably less than their all."

"Well, fuck, it had been a year and a half," replied Grohl. "Of course we were burnt! We thought, 'Okay, so, after Phoenix we can go home!', and there were two ways it could have gone. It could have been the most energetic, out-of-control performance we've ever put on. Or, we could have just stood there and enjoyed the huge audience. We just stood there!"

Suffering a severe case of roadburn, the Foos limped off tour, and returned to their long-neglected domestic lives. But there was a painful reckoning awaiting Grohl, as his relationship with wife Jennifer Youngblood began to unravel. The source of their split—which he described as not acrimonious, if initially awkward—was that he had married too young, reeling from the pain and madness of Nirvana's final days, and perhaps clinging to their relationship as a calm harbor from the storm. "It was horrifying," he told *Classic Rock*'s Ben Mitchell. "I was a fucking kid, and people were dying, and overdosing, and...It was like being a child actor, or something. That can fuck you up for the rest of your life. I just hid in the suburbs of Seattle with my girl, and had barbecues with our friends who had nothing to do with the music scene at all."

But while the relationship had delivered much needed succor and comfort during that earlier time, it soon became a casualty of Grohl's new life as frontman of Foo Fighters, and all that entailed. "I like a good weirdo, and she was one," Grohl later told *Elle* magazine. "We were weird together; we got caught up in romance, the thrill of adulthood. But it wasn't meant to be."

In November 1996, Grohl moved out of the home the couple had shared, the marriage all but over. He was, for all intents and purposes, homeless, and would stay that way for months to follow, leading a dirtbag, vagabond lifestyle as he sofa-surfed and crashed in the spare room of former Scream bandmate Pete Stahl, his bed a well-worn sleeping bag he carried along for his travels. As if that weren't grim enough for a big-time rock star, on occasion he'd awake in the middle of the night to find Stahl's dog pissing on him.

Opposite: Foo Fighters' appearance at the 1996 Phoenix Festival in Stratford-upon-Avon in the UK, ended the touring for the first album on a bum note.

Not that he had much spare time to wallow in his domestic dysfunction. As of November 18, Grohl was focused primarily on Foo Fighters' second album—their first as a group—at Bear Creek Studios, in Woodinville, Washington. In contrast to the sessions that had created the debut—a tornado of activity, Grohl cutting most tracks by himself in under a week—this second album would be produced more in the manner of a big-time rock release, under the tutelage of a big-name rock producer. As well as boasting a sound and set-up that's attracted the likes of Soundgarden, Modest Mouse, and even James Brown, Bear Creek is a residential studio renowned for the warmth and comfort of its environs—and, considering Grohl's most recent digs were a piss-stained sleeping bag, it must have seemed palatial by comparison.

Grohl had selected Gil Norton as producer of *The Colour and the Shape*, a Liverpudlian whose résumé included artists as diverse as Scouse doom-poppers Echo & The Bunnymen, Aussie underdogs The Triffids, underground genii Pere Ubu, and fiery Rhode Island quartet Throwing Muses. But it was Norton's work with the Pixies that had won Grohl's attention, in particular his production on the group's 1991 swansong, *Trompe le Monde*. Fronted by singer/guitarist Black Francis, Pixies' brutish but beautiful songs swung on a switchblade-like quiet/loud axis, a dynamic that saw many predict them as the band to escape the underground, and drag the scene into the mainstream (a fate which, of course, ultimately befell Nirvana). Norton produced their last three albums—before their dissolution in 1993. They later reformed in 2004—but it was this one that particularly intrigued Grohl.

Befuddling some critics and long-term fans upon release, *Trompe le Monde* invited ex-Beefheart keyboard/bass player Eric Drew Feldman into the group's orbit. The resulting sound was, on the surface, more poppy and easily absorbed than the tequila-soaked churn of yore, but underneath the sugary surface, wild mathematics and avant-garde technique were operating. And it was this that suckered in Grohl, and which he wanted to apply to the songs of Foo Fighters' second album. "I love the way you can hear the band falling apart, getting scattered, shooting off in a million different directions," Grohl later said—words he may later have regretted.

Grohl began work with Norton in a hotel room, pulling apart the new songs he'd been writing on the road and jamming with the band during soundcheck, paring them back to their very essences, and putting them back in new, more pleasing shapes. Norton was by no means a passive producer, and he wasn't cowed by the fame of his new client, which suited Grohl: he wanted someone who would help him make those songs better, who would push him to new heights, and not take any bullshit or second-rate material.

However, when the band reconvened at Bear Creek during the winter of 1996, recording early versions of these tracks, the train swiftly vacated the rails. By all accounts, throughout the sessions Norton maintained the exacting standards he'd placed upon Grohl during preproduction with the rest of the band. "He had me doing like forty fucking takes in a row to get it perfect," Grohl later recalled to Marc Maron, presenter of the podcast *WTF!*, who interviewed Grohl in 2013. Nate and William were less experienced in the art of record-making, however. Sunny Day Real Estate's albums had been cut at breakneck speed, on tight budgets, where "good enough" was the by-word (and, to be fair, on the example of those albums "good enough" was pretty fucking great indeed). Now though, they were playing in the big league, under heavy pressure of following up a smash hit debut, by a producer who, it is alleged, called them "the rhythmless section" on at least one occasion. This did not cultivate a positive vibe within the ranks.

The pressure was greatest upon Goldsmith, sticksman in a group fronted by perhaps the most iconic drummer of his generation. (Grohl's ingenious opening snare-and-kick licks on "Teen Spirit" are as instantly recognizable as Clapton's first licks on "Layla.") He struggled under Norton's gaze, sometimes being asked to replay the same parts dozens of times, never really to satisfaction. "William was young, and he was overshadowed by Dave's history," Norton reflected, years later. "As much as I tried to encourage him and guide him, sometimes as a musician the problem is all in your head, not your ability."

Grohl had faced similar challenges while recording Nirvana's *Nevermind* with producer Butch Vig, who made Dave play to a click track when he couldn't stop speeding up while playing "Lithium." In 2016, Vig revealed: "Years later, Dave told me that that broke his heart. He thought, 'Am I gonna be replaced

> "William was young, and he was overshadowed by Dave's history. As much as I tried to encourage him and guide him, sometimes as a musician the problem is all in your head, not your ability."
>
> **GIL NORTON**

Left: Grohl (L) and William Goldsmith (R) hang with Bowie sideman Zachary Alford (center) at David Bowie's 50th birthday celebration concert in New York.

Right: Louise Post of Veruca Salt became Dave Grohl's paramour, following his split from his wife, and helped inspire "Everlong."

by a machine?' But we ran it with the click track and he played it perfectly in one take, and it blew my mind. Like, 'Fuck, is he a good drummer.'" It was there, perhaps, that Grohl learned that high standards and hard work were crucial ingredients in making a brilliant record—even a brilliant punk rock record.

The sessions broke for Christmas, and Grohl repaired to his mother's house in Virginia. It would prove a dark Yuletide for Grohl, who received divorce papers from Jennifer Youngblood in mid-December while at Bear Creek. During the downtime, when not dwelling upon how the album seemed to be slipping away from him, and how the band he'd cultivated over the last eighteen months seemed to be coming asunder, he turned his attention to his broken marriage; to all he'd lost, the pain that he'd caused and the pain he'd sustained, and how there didn't seem to be an emotionally painless solution.

In one of these bleak funks, a song presented itself to Grohl, with the same kind of instantaneous magic "This Is A Call" had while he was in Ireland a couple of years before. The song was a pocket epic, in its four minutes and ten seconds a symphonic sequence of moods, from bruised introspection (and a riff Grohl modestly swore he'd stolen somewhere from Sonic Youth) to surging, speaker-shaking catharsis.

Its lyric was a similarly canny and economic sprawl of longing and love: the pain of things going wrong, and the blind devotion to go down with the sinking ship, to refuse to acknowledge that it's over when, obviously, it's over; and all the collateral damage sustained during the melee. If the lyrics of the debut album were all veils and deflection, out of necessity, now Dave Grohl was telling things as they were for the same reason, to hold on to his sanity, and to find some way out of this mess, with his mind and his dignity intact. The song was about his break-up with Jennifer, sure. But there was a nugget of hope in there, too, inspired by Grohl's newfound love: Louise Post, singer and guitarist with Chicago indie-rock band Veruca Salt.

The song would set the tone for the rest of the album and all the confessions contained within. Even Bob Dylan loved it, and once told Grohl he'd love to cover it. The song is "Everlong," and Dave Grohl wrote it in forty-five minutes, and it's still perhaps the greatest song he's ever written.

"Everlong" proved that, even in the midst of darkness, salvation could be found. But the Foo Fighters' second album was a ship still sorely in need of righting. After recording an acoustic demo of "Everlong" and another of the new album's finer songs, "Walking After You," at WGNS Studio in Washington, D.C. over the Christmas break, the group reassembled at Hollywood's Grandmaster Recorders—a storied recording studio with a foreboding quote from Shakespeare's *A Midsummer Night's Dream*: "What fools these mortals be!" daubed on its exterior—in February 1997. To be more accurate, Grandmaster Recorders hosted the group, minus William Goldsmith.

During the Christmas break, Grohl had listened to the extant sessions over and over again, a gnawing sense of doubt setting in. Talking with Pat Smear, his oldest friend among the Foo Fighters, he confided his feelings that the band's performances simply weren't cutting it. Norton concurred, and encouraged

Grohl to rerecord the drum parts for one song from the album, "Monkey Wrench," himself.

The results were, for Grohl and Norton, revelatory, though Norton worked Grohl every bit as hard as he had Goldsmith: "Fucking noon 'til midnight," Grohl told Maron. "I looked like Arnold Schwarzenegger by the end of that day, and I told him, like, 'What are you fucking hearing that I'm not hearing, dude?'" Swiftly, they set about rerecording further drum tracks. Soon, Grohl had recut most, if not all, of the drum parts himself (Goldsmith's performances ultimately remained intact on "Doll" and parts of "Up In Arms," and "My Poor Brain"). For Grohl, the decision was a no-brainer: his priority was making the best record he could, and, in the face of the earlier lackluster sessions, these freshly recorded drum parts delivered the sound he wanted to hear.

For Goldsmith, however, the news that he had been erased from the majority of tracks on the new album would prove humiliating and heartbreaking. For what it was worth, Grohl didn't want Goldsmith to leave the band; he wanted Goldsmith with the group as they toured the new album and, presumably, to drum on the next Foo Fighters record. But Grohl's drum parts would remain on the second album. Nevertheless, as sessions drew to a close, Goldsmith made clear that he was exiting the group, citing both the group's workload—much heavier than Grohl had suggested it would be when he joined—along with lingering ill feeling over the second album.

"William didn't want to go on tour, and he wanted to play with other people," Grohl told *Kerrang!* in 1997, upon the album's release. "There's no serious animosity, but it sucks."

Goldsmith was the first casualty of *The Colour and the Shape*, but Grohl and his Foo Fighters were reluctant to spend too much time mourning William's absence. For one thing, they had a mighty new album to celebrate, an album that built on the blueprint Grohl had set on his lonesome with the debut, with a confidence that obscured its traumatic birth. The dynamism that had characterized the first Foos LP returned, more muscular and steroidal this time around, Grohl carving tunes that stopped and started and lurched and leapt with kinetic fury. Tunes that ranged from the gleeful abandon of "Monkey Wrench" to the angular math-metal of "Hey, Johnny Park!" And from

Right: Following Goldsmith's exit from the band, Grohl welcomed aboard the drummer he'd later recognize as the brother he never had, Taylor Hawkins (far right).

This Is A Blackout

Foo Fighters, 1997. The mood within the band improved immeasurably following Taylor's arrival—but the line-up would soon change once more.

> "Nirvana were my favorite band in the world at that time, and I was convinced Dave would think I was a dork. But he came up and introduced himself to me, and was really fucking nice, really complimentary, just a really nice cat."
>
> **TAYLOR HAWKINS**

Left: Pat Smear at the MTV Video Music Awards that marked his farewell as a Foo Fighter, alongside MTV *House of Style* co-presenter Cindy Crawford

the ticking-timebomb quiet/LOUD explosions of "My Poor Brain" to the rising-from-the-mire anthem of "My Hero" and its surging, plummeting-airliner thrills. Alone, Grohl had wrangled a fearsome punk din on Foo Fighters' debut; emboldened by his bandmates on the follow-up, Foo Fighters sounded like a real, live band—like Pinocchio changed from puppet to flesh and blood—and much of *The Colour and the Shape* captures their might up-close and personal. They sound loud. They sound massive. They sound marvelous.

That sound, meanwhile, was lent depth and meaning by Grohl's lyrics. The album shifts through a series of moods, from the joyfulness of "Monkey Wrench," to the chirpy spite of "Up In Arms," to the slow-burning melancholy of "Everlong," to the bittersweet longing of "Walking After You," but these songs mostly compose a single story from multiple viewpoints: that of Grohl's break-up from Youngblood. For all the carefree slamdance of its riff, "Monkey Wrench" plunged its hands deep into the maw of the break-up, the contradictions of love and loss, Grohl later admitting it was about "realizing that you are the source of all the problems in a relationship, and you love the other person so much you want to free them of the problem, which is actually yourself." To truly love Youngblood, "Monkey Wrench" seems to suggest, Grohl had to let her go. The monkey wrench was him. "I was the one who left you" runs the refrain to "Up In Arms," but the song's narrator sure seems to be the brokenhearted one, the one who can't move on; "February Stars" is another dispatch from the depths of the darkness, "Hanging on here until I'm gone."

The full spectrum of love and its fallout played across thirteen tracks, even the ones not directly influenced by Grohl's divorce, like "My Hero," a track written early in the group's lifespan and played on their first tours, which many critics and interviewers quickly took as a tribute to Kurt Cobain but was, as Grohl would later explain, dedicated to the people who'd truly inspired him: not the rock stars whose posters decorated his childhood walls, but teachers, parents, softball coaches, family friends. Foo Fighters' music was hardly earthbound, but *The Colour and the Shape*—its title inspired by the group's tour manager, Peter, who would pick up random gifts he didn't need wherever the band traveled (candles, lamps, a bowling pin), seduced by, of course, their color and shape—was mature, and had its feet planted firmly on the ground.

Compare *The Colour and the Shape* to the spread of guitar-oriented music in the era that immediately followed Cobain's suicide and the slow decay of alternative rock: it had little truck with the Britpop of Oasis, which would never translate to the Americas like it dominated its home country, while the pop-punk of Green Day, perhaps grunge's immediate successors in the hearts of the Lollapalooza generation, came off juvenile, flighty, and insubstantial in comparison. Listen again to "Monkey Wrench" and you hear a song that delivers all of the snotty, kinetic thrills contained within "Basket Case" or, indeed, any track by the punk rockers who followed Green Day into the charts—Rancid, Offspring et al. But you can hear so much more: a metallic muscle, a desire to crank amps to eleven and smash shit up, an emotional content perhaps beyond your typical mall-dwelling twelve-year-old. *The Colour and the Shape* possessed a most sophisticated rock lexicon, drawing upon the rhythmic angularity of underground rock and nineties post-hardcore, allied to a gift for melody that was never frivolous, with a soupcon of metallic brawn, a touch of Beatles-style grace. The album belonged to no single genre, betraying ambitions the group would further realize on later releases.

On his first swing as a bandleader in the big leagues, Grohl had delivered a masterpiece. Though he'd paid dearly for it, too. And the hits would just keep on coming.

As he readied the album for release, Grohl found himself in a familiar position: he had to assemble musicians to play the music he'd just recorded. At least this time there was just one space within the ranks to fill: that of drummer. And Grohl knew who he wanted to occupy the newly vacant Foos drum stool: a young, ridiculously talented, absurdly enthusiastic sticksman who was at that time playing with an artist bigger, hotter, and more successful than the Foos.

"I've always wanted to be in a band," Taylor Hawkins told *Rhythm* magazine in November 1998. A Texas-born, California-raised shock of sinew and toothy grin who taught himself drums playing along to albums by Queen and The Police, Hawkins looked and still looks like Dave Grohl's younger brother, amplifying Grohl's untrammeled devotion, zeal, and intensity; according to Dave himself, Hawkins is also a finer drummer than Grohl. After graduating high school, Hawkins pummeled skins for SoCal psychedelic prog metallers Sylvia and backed Canadian rocker Sass Jordan, before taking the drum stool with the prodigious Ottawan singer-songwriter Alanis Morissette.

By the time Taylor began working with Morissette, her third solo album, 1995's *Jagged Little Pill*, was sent chartwards by hit singles like "You Oughta Know" (a righteous, vengeful break-up song rendered unforgettable by Alanis's memory of going down on her ex in the cinema), "One Hand In My Pocket," and "Head Over Feet," witty, heartfelt pop with a grungy edge. Following the smash success of one of its weakest songs, "Ironic," the album went on to sell sixteen million copies in the US alone, and shifting thirty-three million units across the globe. And, as Alanis traveled that globe, bringing the songs to the people, Taylor crossed paths with Dave on the European festival circuit. Impressed by Hawkins's energetic playing and his amiable manner, Grohl almost instantly sensed a kindred spirit, along with a motherfucker of a drummer.

"We did a couple of shows together in Europe," Taylor remembered in 2005. "Nirvana were my favorite band in the world at that time, and I was convinced Dave would think I was a dork. But he came up and introduced himself to me, and was really fucking nice, really complimentary, just a really nice cat."

Right: Franz Stahl, who would replace Pat Smear as Foo Fighters guitarist. He and Grohl had played together before, in punk group Scream.

"By 1998, I would sit down to do an interview and people would ask, 'Okay, who's in the fuckin' band now? Has anybody left in the last month-and-a-half?'"

DAVE GROHL

"My first impression of Taylor was that he was just this fuckin' crazy partying surfer," Grohl added. "Which was absolutely correct."

So when it became clear Goldsmith wanted out of Foo Fighters, Grohl realized fast who he wanted in. Grohl imagined Hawkins wouldn't want to ditch his lucrative gig with Morissette, perhaps not realizing Hawkins was already one of Grohl's biggest fans, telling *Rhythm* magazine in 1996, "He's fucking ridiculous. . . I love the simplicity and beauty of his playing. The fills that he does are damn great." Eighteen months into his stint as drummer-for-hire with Morissette, Hawkins was ready to find himself a home in a real, actual band.

"When I read that Will was quitting Foo Fighters, or being fired or whatever," Hawkins remembered, "I got hold of Dave through another friend, and I said to him, 'Yo, I heard you're looking for a drummer,' and he said, 'Yeah, you know anybody?' [laughs] Cocksucker! He made me ask. . . Actually, in his mind, he thought since Alanis was one of the biggest things in the world at the time, and Foo Fighters were still just kinda starting out he was like, 'Why would you want to bail on someone who's selling thirty million records?' But I wanted to play rock music, and I loved the Foo Fighters—they were my favorite fucking band."

Hawkins was swiftly installed upon the Foo Fighters drum stool where, very quickly, it felt like he'd always been. And in his new boss, Hawkins found a new best friend. "Taylor and I are like brothers," Grohl said later. "The two of us are like best friends. You only find so many best friends in a lifetime. Taylor and I wound up being separated at birth."

So surely now the tumult that had been shaking the Foo Fighters—and Dave Grohl's young life—would calm down?

Well, what do you think?

September 4, 1997 finds Foo Fighters stood atop the marquee of New York City's Radio City Music Hall, as fans pack the pavement of Sixth Avenue in anticipation of a most special performance as part of that year's MTV Music Awards. Lean from four months touring America and Europe in support of *The Colour and the Shape*, the Foos frug like well-drilled commandos, blitzing through a taut "Monkey Wrench" from behind the venue's iconic neon-lit sign—to the delight of passer-by Manhattanites and four buses packed with tourists. And when the group make a second appearance upon the Marquee later on in the awards show, Pat Smear—dressed in a fetching designer-camouflage long-coat—takes the microphone, and announces: "The last song we played was my last song with the band. I would like to introduce you to Franz Stahl, who will be taking over. Thank you. Rock on guys! FOO FIGHTERS!"

And so ends Pat Smear's tenure with the group. Smear had announced his desire to quit Foo Fighters six months earlier, during Taylor Hawkins' first rehearsal with the group, citing exhaustion, a desire to escape the touring life—and a wish to pursue a TV career as presenter of MTV fashion show *House of Style* alongside supermodel Cindy Crawford. He wanted to leave immediately, but Grohl—who begged Smear to stay in the band—managed to convince him to remain for six weeks' promotional duties, a grace period which ultimately stretched to half a year. "Pat said, 'I think you guys should be a three-piece,'" remembered Grohl to *Melody Maker*'s Dave Simpson. "He just didn't want to be in the band anymore. He didn't like touring—he really fucking hated flying and just wanted to stay at home. A lot of it had to do with the fact that we're always working. He wanted to do other stuff, and I totally understand that. But I look at this band as my little baby, and I want to see it grow up in front of me."

Grohl later said that his first instinct upon learning of Smear's desire to quit was to call Franz Stahl, his former bandmate from Scream. Grohl had known Stahl since he was sixteen years old; Stahl had pretty much taught Grohl the finer points of playing guitar and writing songs. "He's like a brother to me," Grohl told *Kerrang!* "So now I feel safe, looking over and knowing that here's this incredible musician who's like a family member to me." Stahl was playing shows in Japan with 'J-rock' legend J (Jun Onose) of Luna Sea, when Grohl reached out to him, and he flew back to the US within hours to join the Foos' ranks. He'd had a day's rehearsal with the group when he joined them at Radio City Music Hall. It wasn't just Stahl's friendship with Grohl that made him a logical choice to join the band; Dave would later explain that songs like "Monkey Wrench" and "Enough Space" were written in Stahl's image, and that Grohl would have invited Stahl to join the Foos from day one, had he not been fronting his own band Wool at the time.

Stahl's presence lent a new stability to the group that Grohl said had approached the earlier shows in support of

The Colour and the Shape on somewhat shaky form, with Pat Smear's imminent exit souring the usual bonhomie between the members. Indeed, Grohl later admitted that his friendship with Smear all but broke down during this period, telling *Recovery* magazine in 2000 that "the last time we saw each other we almost got into a fight," suggesting that the reasons for Smear's leaving the Foos ran deeper than he'd previously hinted. "What do you do when you go through a divorce and one of your band members decides to quit the band because he likes his wife better than you do? You start thinking, 'OK, well, I think I wanna kick your ass'."

This new-look Foo Fighters would go on to play a further 118 shows together across the next two years—years Stahl would later describe as the best of his life. But the group almost ran adrift again early in 1998, as another key cog within the Foo Fighters machine made plans to exit the group.

"By 1998, I would sit down to do an interview and people would ask, 'Okay, who's in the fuckin' band now? Has anybody left in the last month-and-a-half?'," Grohl laughs in the excellent 2011 rockumentary *Foo Fighters: Back and Forth*. "But there was always Nate." But the Foos' mainstay bassplayer felt conflicted loyalties, as a tentative reunion with his Sunny Day Real Estate bandmates grew from conversations to compiling a posthumous set of rarities, to recording an album of new material, and taking to the road together again. Indeed, in the weeks running up to the recording sessions in spring 1998, Mendel seriously considered quitting the Foo Fighters to rejoin Goldsmith, Enigk and Hoerner for the album that would become their comeback set, *How It Feels to Be Something On*. Indeed, Mendel went as far as to call Grohl and tell him he was exiting the group.

Mendel now describes his mindset towards Sunny Day Real Estate during those days as "high school crush-irrational," and that the moment he put the phone down he realized his true place was alongside Grohl in the Foos. As he stewed over his bad decision, Grohl went with his old school-buddy Jimmy Swanson to Ribsters—clearly a fine dining establishment of high repute—and got "fucking shit-faced," wrecking his rental car and ending up in his old bedroom at his mom's house in Virginia, where she woke him at 7am with news that a tearful Mendel was on the phone, withdrawing his resignation. Disaster, for once, had been averted.

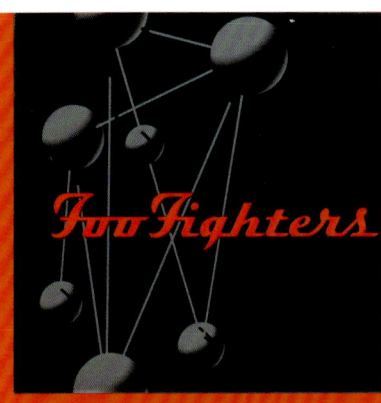

The Colour and the Shape

Released: May 20, 1997
Label: Roswell/Capitol
Recorded: November–December, 1996 and January–February, 1997
 Bear Creek Studios, Woodinville, Washington, D.C
 WGNS Studios, Washington, D.C.
 Grandmaster Recorders, Hollywood, California

PERSONNEL:
Dave Grohl: lead vocals, rhythm guitar, drums
Pat Smear: lead guitar
Nate Mendel: bass

Additional personnel:
William Goldsmith: drums on "Doll", "Up in Arms" (credited for slow intro), "My Poor Brain" (verses only, uncredited), "The Colour And The Shape" (uncredited), and "Down In The Park" (uncredited)
Taylor Hawkins: drums on "Requiem," "Drive Me Wild," and "Baker Street" (tenth anniversary edition's bonus tracks only)
Gil Norton: production

TRACK LISTING:
All tracks written by Dave Grohl, Nate Mendel, and Pat Smear except where noted

1. "Doll"
2. "Monkey Wrench"
3. "Hey, Johnny Park!"
4. "My Poor Brain"
5. "Wind Up"
6. "Up In Arms"
7. "My Hero"
8. "See You"
9. "Enough Space" (Grohl)
10. "February Stars"
11. "Everlong" (Grohl)
12. "Walking After You" (Grohl)
13. "New Way Home"

Bonus tracks (Tenth anniversary edition)
14. "Requiem" (Killing Joke cover)
15. "Drive Me Wild" (Vanity 6 cover)
16. "Down In The Park" (Gary Numan and Tubeway Army cover)
17. "Baker Street" (Gerry Rafferty cover)
18. "Dear Lover"
19. "The Colour And The Shape'

Grohl announces his commitment to his group through the ancient art of tattooing.

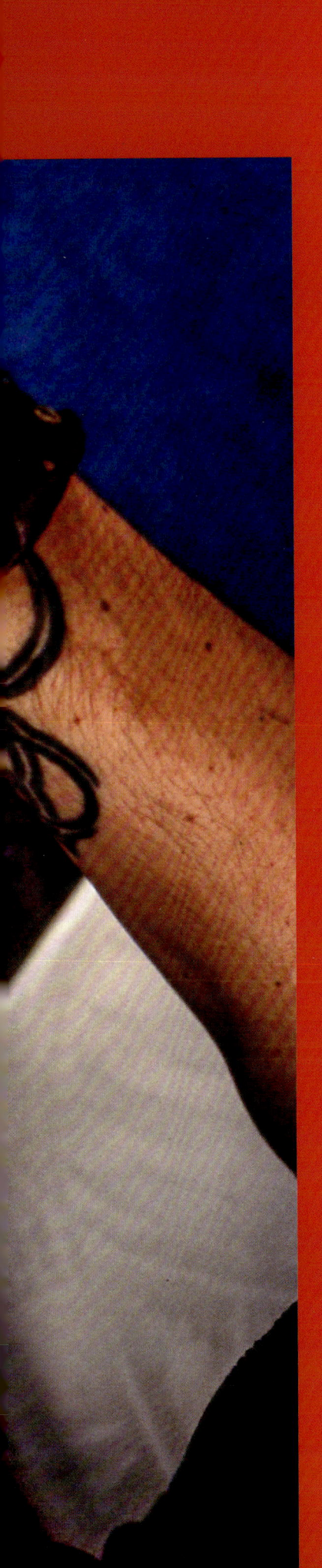

Learn To Fly

"The last album was kind of depressing. It had a lot to do with the demise of a relationship. Two-and-a-half years later, I had to learn how to live life again, and 'Learn To Fly' is that search for things to make you feel alive and keep you exploring."

DAVE GROHL

Foo Fighters: The Band That Dave Made

Learn To Fly

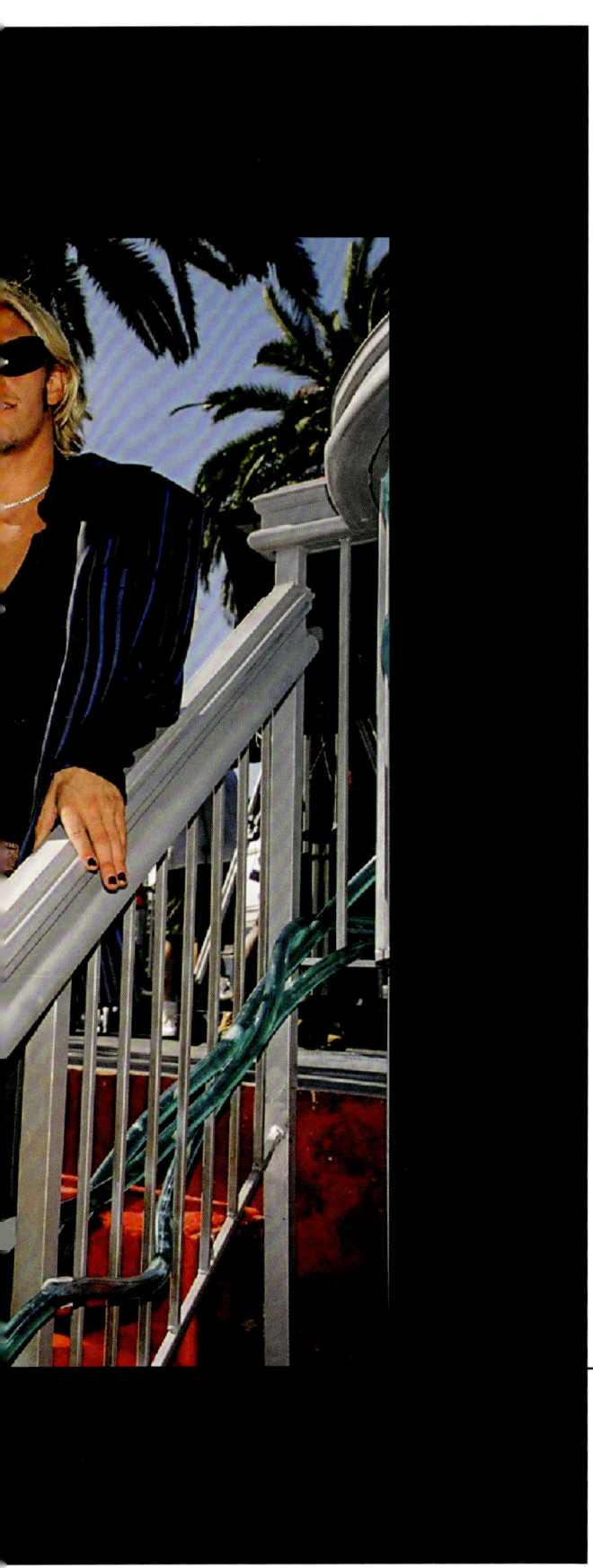

For all the turbulence behind the scenes and unrest within the band's line-up, it was with *The Colour and the Shape* that Foo Fighters hit their stride; Grohl would later say that, after the album was released, all the things that happen to the hot new bands you see in the magazines began to happen for them. Certainly, *The Colour and the Shape* was where all the press interest that had followed the group since they were a mere music industry rumor was translated into actual sales, and they became a phenomenon in their own right. The in-depth interviews, magazine covers, and television coverage that the band had "enjoyed" in their early days had been, to a sizable degree, thanks to Grohl's extant celebrity from his days with Nirvana; the anticipation that he might share tantalizing gossip and information about that band, which still so intrigued their fans and the wider world, sold magazines. But it was with *The Colour and the Shape*, and the success that followed, that the Foos' own juggernaut phenomenon caught up with Nirvana's outsized media presence.

They had videos on MTV all the time now, Grohl noted. And what videos—inspired, comedic, and ambitious. For "Monkey Wrench," Grohl returned to his apartment from grocery shopping, only to find it chain-locked from the inside, and another, black-clad Grohl and his Foo Fighters rocking out in his front-room, to the exasperation of the first Grohl, peeking in via the peephole. The first Grohl's neighbors, another Pat, Nate and Taylor, soon join him in watching the band through the letterbox, before smashing their way into the apartment and rockin' away themselves, as *another* batch of Foos watch on. Inception had nothing on this. For "Everlong," filmmaker Michel Gondry—later known for movies like *Eternal Sunshine of the Spotless Mind* and *Be Kind Rewind*—filmed the dream-sequence of a slumbering Grohl, sleeping peacefully beside his wife (Taylor, in eerily convincing drag), wherein Grohl, bedecked in spiky black hair and "punk" garb as if dressed as Sid Vicious for Halloween, wandered about a raucous house party, only to discover his wife being hassled by a couple of 1950s-style greasers, who Grohl dispatched with a

Left: The Foo Fighters arrive at the 1998 MTV Video Music Awards in California, USA, a year after Franz Stahl (second from left) made his debut with the group.

Above: Director Michel Gondry

Right: Promoting *The Colour and the Shape* on *The Tonight Show With Jay Leno*, February 1998

comedically outsized hand. Taylor, meanwhile, dreams "she" is in a remote shack near a forest, being stalked by those same delinquents, while Grohl picks wood nearby. A rather more literal clip for "My Hero" featured a man running into a blazing building to rescue a baby, a dog, and a beloved photograph, while the Foos play in the wreckage, and the impressionistic promo for "Walking After You"—a rerecorded version now featuring drums, cut for the soundtrack to the first big-screen offshoot of TV's *The X-Files*—saw Grohl and his lover (played by actress Arly Jover) separated by a plate-glass divide, during visiting time at a prison.

Back in the era when MTV actually played music videos, these short films enjoyed the kind of heavy rotation that had flung Nirvana to stardom a few years earlier. But they weren't the only measure of the Foos' encroaching eminence. *The Colour and the Shape* was a bona fide chart hit, reaching the US *Billboard* Top 10, and Top 3 in the UK, certified platinum with 2.3 million copies sold in the US alone, while the album was nominated for the Best Rock Album Grammy, with "Monkey Wrench" tipped for Best Hard Rock Performance.

The touring in support of *The Colour and the Shape*, meanwhile, climaxed with a return to Little John's Farm in Reading, the scene of their 1995 triumph. And while the Foos weren't quite headliners yet—playing fourth on the bill, beneath Beastie Boys, The Prodigy, and Supergrass—they'd escaped the tent for the main stage, and redeemed themselves,

Learn To Fly

following the lackluster Phoenix Festival set that had ended the touring for the debut album. Surviving footage from the afternoon sees Grohl and his Foos kick-starting a moshpit that stretches back as far as the sound-desk with the inspired lurch of "For All The Cows," while a raw-nerved "Everlong" proved Grohl could inject such grandiose, big-scale rock events with an unguarded emotion, and make them moments to truly remember. And for all that the lyrics to "This Is A Call" might've been mostly nonsense, by Grohl's own admission, the Reading crowd scream every one of them back at the Foos with a fury and devotion that impresses.

This gleeful Reading appearance saw the Foos disembark the touring juggernaut on a high, having seemingly proved that even a year of heavy turmoil could not undermine their resolve, and that the line-up changes and seismic emotional adjustments that had recently characterized the band were now behind them. In truth, however, Dave Grohl headed into his well-earned break in the uncomfortable knowledge that things had to change: in his private life, in his group's relationship with the industry they operated in—and once again within the group's own ranks.

As far as the world's media is concerned, beyond his fearsome skills as a singer and a songwriter, beyond his god-of-thunder might behind a drumkit, Dave Grohl's defining

> "I'd been living in LA for about a year and a half, just being a drunk, getting fucked up every night and doing horrible shit, and I finally got sick of that. I was like, 'I've gotta go back to Virginia or I'll fucking die in this place.'"
>
> **DAVE GROHL**

characteristic is his "niceness." There are many reasons why Dave is considered "nice," not least the fact that Grohl is, in the least cynical manner possible, a "pro" when it comes to interacting with the media. Sit down to interview Dave and you swiftly know you are in the company of a man who understands why he is there; no shrinking violet (though also no self-publicizing egoist), Dave comes to the table with anecdotes, opinions, bonhomie, and an unguarded engagement with the matter at hand. He might have spent the months promoting Foo Fighters' first album mostly deflecting invasive questions about Nirvana and Kurt—and the months promoting the Foos' second album similarly avoiding questions about his freshly ended marriage, the ex-bandmates who'd fled the group, and the current details of his private life. But he did so with a grace that the interviewers often didn't deserve, and there's little chance they didn't leave the confab without a story to share with their readers.

Furthermore, Grohl is, by his own admission, not much of a party animal, the odd grief-fueled misadventure in a rental car notwithstanding. He's never touched coke, speed, or smack, and hasn't smoked a joint or dropped acid in decades. In an X-rated rock world, he's unabashedly "suitable for all audiences." He won't bite the head off a bat, spike the punch with illicit chemicals, or try to get off with your little sister. Grohl is a nice guy, and if some in the media sometimes mistake that "niceness" for being boring, that's just testament to their own paucity of imagination.

The problems arise when Grohl struggles to live up to that reputation. The man is, after all, only human. In the 2011 rockumentary *Foo Fighters: Back and Forth*, Grohl reflected on Goldsmith's ouster from the band and reflected, ruefully, "It was a weird time, and I was young. What the fuck." You sense that, in this moment, Grohl knows people will perceive him as having fallen short of the unreal expectations they expect him to conform to. The problems arise when we expect a man to not be able to make mistakes, when none of us is perfect. Let the man have some regrets. How is he supposed to learn?

As the Foos parted ways for some much-needed rest and recuperation, Grohl returned to a private life that was very much in transition, as he weathered the aftershocks of the post-traumatic confusion following Kurt's death, and the end of the marriage he rushed into in search of stability and safety. His relationship with Louise Post had foundered early in 1997 and, according to legend, ended via telephone just before a disastrous Veruca Salt gig characterized by a drunken and remorseful performance by an emotional Post. The rumor mill then whispered that Grohl proceeded to date actress Winona Ryder (a rumor Grohl denied), and the nascent proliferation of what Grohl later described as "internet gossipy trash sites" went on to imagine him in trysts with a string of starlets, gossip he refused to dignify with a serious reply.

By his own admission, however, Grohl was tiring of life in Los Angeles. "I'd been living in LA for about a year and a half, just being a drunk, getting fucked up every night and doing horrible shit," he told *Kerrang!*'s Morat, "and I finally got sick of that." By the standards of most of the wasted denizens of the Sunset Strip, it's hard not to imagine that Grohl was a comparative choir-boy. "My party life was, like, having a barbecue in my backyard, or maybe once a week going into a bar and drinking a bottle of Tequila," he told *Recovery* magazine. But he knew when something wasn't working, and his life in Los Angeles had hit a wall. Grohl was ready to bail on life as an eligible rock star bachelor, on Hollywood bar life; ready to go MIA. He needed a change. And, in a sense, he needed to come home again.

Opposite: Dave Grohl, c. late 1990s. By 1998 Grohl had already been through major changes, both in private and within his band.

"I was like, 'I've gotta go back to Virginia or I'll fucking die in this place,'" he told Morat. And so, back to Virginia he went.

It wasn't just turning the corner on his dissolute LA days that drew Grohl to the wilds of Virginia; he was still licking the wounds of the Foos' bruising first taste of the Big Budget Music Industry Experience. *The Colour and the Shape* had proved a smash success, and it had to be, as sessions across three separate locations—each a well-regarded, state-of-the-art recording studio—had also made it a very expensive album, with a swollen budget the band had to recoup. You could build your own studio for a fraction of what that album had cost, and then you'd be operating on your own timetable, without having to worry about the clock ticking on, like the world's most expensive taxi cab.

So that's exactly what Grohl did. He bought a great big house on Nicholson Lane in Alexandria, Virginia, not far from where he'd gone to school as a kid, and in the basement he began building what would be his first recording studio of his own. It was rustic, rudimentary, about as far removed from the plush environs he'd recently experienced as possible, with sleeping bags hanging on the walls as insulation and sound-proofing. The studio, which he christened "Studio 606," was analogue and proudly so. Indeed, the API board had belonged to Allen Sides, founder of the renowned Nashville studio Ocean Way; it was rumored that Lynyrd Skynyrd themselves had recorded on it. The studio possessed none of the gadgetry then taking hold of the music industry, which at first presented its own challenges, but soon seemed perfectly in tune with an album that would be as richly timeless as a gorgeous seventies stereo system with wood veneer, silver finishing, and more illuminated VUs than, well, Grohl's home-made studio.

Grohl loved his new digs. It wasn't just the recording studio in the mancave; the move to Alexandria marked a serious change of gears from his period in Los Angeles. "Living in LA for a year and a half had ignited that hatred I had for so long for things that are false and glamorous and just not 'real,'" Grohl said in a promotional documentary he shot for Foo Fighters' third album, which he recorded in Alexandria. "Getting back to Virginia, there was just a nice feeling of community, a music scene, old friends and things that I'd never lost but felt like I needed more of in my life." This change of pace would inspire a song for the new album, "Ain't It The Life," a gorgeous country-rock number with swooning tremolo guitar that sounded like the end of another chilled day in Virginia. The angst that had driven *The Colour and the Shape* had dissipated, and the songs Grohl would record for this third album reflected that. "Ain't It The Life," meanwhile, was a song Grohl said he would "love to play on my porch." It certainly wasn't the work of a man living out of a piss-stained sleeping bag in his friend's basement.

Sessions for this new album began in March 1999, and Grohl noted that these marked the first recordings where the group entered the studio with very little new material already demoed; much of the new album would be written while they were recording, a luxury afforded by possessing their own studio. Still, this had not been Grohl's initial plan; earlier that year he'd booked a room at Barco Rebar, a modest rehearsal space in nearby Falls Church, not far from where Grohl had auditioned to join Scream years before. The

Opposite: *There Is Nothing Left to Lose* would be completed by the Foo Fighters core trio. (L-R) Dave Grohl, Taylor Hawkins, and Nate Mendel.

> "... as we were writing songs for the new record, we were doing something far beyond anything we'd imagined. Franz is a great player, and a really great friend. But this album is really important to us, and we felt like we wanted to go in as confident and as focused as possible."
>
> **DAVE GROHL**

plan had been for the quartet to jam on new song ideas, play with some fresh riffs, to try and fashion some tuneage for the forthcoming sessions; much of *The Colour and the Shape*'s material had begun in a similar fashion, albeit with a much different line-up.

But these rehearsals at Barco Rebar would prove fateful for Franz Stahl. The Foos would rehearse and kick the new ideas around for a week or so, then break for a month, before regrouping to work on the new material some more, repeating this process several times. Grohl, Mendel and Hawkins proved productive during this period, pulling "Aurora," one of the finer songs from the forthcoming album, together from out of nowhere during one such jam session. But Grohl noticed that Stahl was struggling to keep up during these rehearsals, and that somehow the chemistry was lacking when he was playing with them. With memories of the grinding sessions for *The Colour and the Shape* still fresh in his mind, and William Goldsmith's messy exit from the group, Grohl discussed his reservations over Stahl with Nate and Taylor, and when they agreed that things weren't jelling with Stahl, Grohl realized he had to ask his old friend—the man who helped teach him to play guitar and to write songs—to leave the band.

With Smear's proposal of a year or so previous—"I think you guys should be a three-piece"—possibly ringing in his ears, Grohl prepared to tell Stahl that Foo Fighters would be progressing as a trio. Stahl was then living in Austin, Texas, and flying to Virginia for the rehearsals. Grohl didn't want Stahl to fly in to discover he was out of the band, and Grohl didn't want to fly to Austin to inform Stahl he was out, as Franz would probably be tipped off by Grohl coming to visit him that something was up. So Grohl essentially fired Stahl by phone, in his mind the least-worst of three bad options.

It didn't go well. Grohl and the remaining Foos told Stahl they were chalking it up to "musical differences." "Everything they were saying to me, there was no validity in any of it," Stahl told Grohl's biographer Paul Brannigan later. "It was complete bullshit." Angered, Stahl flew to Grohl's house, hammering on the door and demanding an explanation, which he found equally as unsatisfying as the one he'd received over the phone. In frustration, Stahl broke down in tears.

It was as ugly a resolution as Grohl could have feared, and as Stahl departed he sensed that one of his oldest, dearest friendships was coming to an end. It was a high price to pay for the future Grohl wanted for his Foo Fighters, for the creative single-mindedness he knew he had to pursue. "But as we were writing songs for the new record, we were doing something far beyond anything we'd imagined," Grohl told *Recovery* magazine. "Franz had a hard time finding his place in that. We said, 'You know, it's probably best that we go and make the record as three people.' Franz is a great player, and a really great friend. But this album is really important to us, and we felt like we wanted to go in as confident and as focused as possible."

The sessions would prove idyllic for Grohl and his newly-shorn Foo Fighters. Sure, they were "focused," but having toiled to distraction over the last album, work on this new record took a more leisurely pace. "It was all about just settling in the next phase of life, that place where I could sit back and relax, because there had been so much crazy shit the past three years," Grohl told *Kerrang!* later, referring both to the sessions for the album, and the themes that ran through the new songs.

The trio who now composed the Foo Fighters had bonded entirely, and an atmosphere of bonhomie pervaded Studio 606 during the sessions. "It was one of the most relaxing times of my whole life," Grohl continued. "All we did was eat chili, drink beer and whiskey, and record whenever we felt like it. When I listen to that record, it totally brings me back to that basement. I remember how it smelled, and how it was in the spring—the windows were open and we'd do vocals until you could hear the birds through the microphone."

As the power trio jammed their new songs into life, these tunes largely avoided the more visceral dynamics and punk rock trappings of the first two albums, owing more to AM Radio than the alternative era. To a large part this was a natural consequence of Grohl and Hawkins's simpatico classic rock tendencies, though it was also a conscious reaction to the times. As the turn of the millennium drew closer, alternative rock had finally lost its grip on the zeitgeist, replaced by a gnarly hybrid of rock instrumentation and rap sonics, later tagged "nu metal." The scene leaders were Korn and Limp Bizkit, with a slew of less-inspired followers trailing in their wake; the groups wore shorts and wild-coloured hair, a look disdainful Glaswegian post-rock wunderkinds Mogwai christened "sports goth," and the lyrical content spanned a spectrum from exorcising childhood abuse, to railing inchoately at the world, to demanding "Nookie."

While that might have thrilled the moshpit massive, Grohl—who had just turned thirty—knew it wasn't his scene, and performed a stylistic left-turn that would sire some of the best songs he's ever written. "The dynamic of popular rock music had become so caveman!" he remembered to *Kerrang!* "I thought, 'Let's write some songs. I'm sick of screaming and I'm sick of my distortion pedal!'"

This more classic, more considered approach was in perfect harmony with the place that Grohl found himself emotionally, and with the lyrics he'd write. The lead single, "Learn To Fly" was of a kin with Boston's "More Than A Feeling," their signature epic of keening vocals, soaring, powerful chords, and glorious seventies guitar heroics. The song had, years earlier, helped inspire the riff to Nirvana's "Smells Like Teen Spirit." But where Kurt changed the chords to set a more uncertain, unsettling and utterly non-triumphant mood, "Learn To Fly" unabashedly channeled the romance and emotion of the original, without flinching that some hipster with face piercings might think the sentiment uncool. Irony was not at play here; as on much of the album. Grohl meant it, man.

The absence of cynicism in his love of classic rock ensured he delivered uplifting melodic rock on a level with its inspirations—and a sense of optimism that befit the lyric's tale of rebirth. It's not hard to read autobiography in Grohl's words, in his tale of reaching for salvation, for redemption, for

Left: *Frampton Comes Alive!*—the album that made the talk box guitar sound famous. Decades later Foo Fighters would adopt it for their song "Generator."

Opposite: Classic seventies band, Boston, *c.*1976. Their melodic, soft-rock vibe influenced *There Is Nothing Left to Lose*.

rebirth, but also needing "a devil to help me get things right." "The song is about the search for something real, something alive, something that's going to make you feel alive," explained Grohl. "The last album was kind of depressing. It had a lot to do with the demise of a relationship, and missing someone and loving someone and understanding that there's no way you can be with this person but there's no way you can be without them. Two-and-a-half years later, I had to learn how to live life again, and 'Learn To Fly' is that search for things to make you feel alive and keep you exploring."

The deliriously romantic "Generator" meanwhile, was similarly indebted to seventies soft rock, its eerie, nagging guitar hook-line foregrounding a special effect immortalized by the best-selling album of 1976. Early predecessors of the talk box—a variant of compression devices like wah-wah pedals—were first developed in 1939, but not released on the mass market until the early seventies. Via a tube feeding from the musician's mouth, the talk box changed the sound of the guitar in accordance with the shape of the guitarist's mouth. The gizmo was perhaps best showcased by former Humble Pie guitarist Peter Frampton, whose ubiquitous 1976 live solo album *Frampton Comes Alive!* played the talk box to the fore on its two smash hit singles, "Show Me The Way" and "Do You Feel Like We Do." "Generator's" lead guitar line was clearly inspired by "Show Me The Way's" unforgettable hook, while Grohl's lyric was one of his most wide-eyed ballads yet, a tribute both to a love and to the redemptive powers of love, Grohl asking "Can't you hear my motored heart? You're the one who started it."

But the finest of *There Is Nothing Left to Lose*'s classic rock trilogy was the aforementioned "Aurora," a vulnerable, stargazing swoon that refracted seventies soft-rock anthemics via the futuristic space-rock constellations of Mogwai; Grohl described it as "the heaviest thing I've ever written." At the song's heart lay an elliptical, delay-treated guitar figure, around which the song built from a hauntingly elemental intro to a grungy approximation of a jangling, Byrdsian folk-rock ballad, and then, with expertly observed pace, to a colossal crescendo which drove up the volume, but never sacrificing its gentle power. There was something affecting and bittersweet to "Aurora's" melody, possessed of hope but also sadness, and so ran the lyric, capturing a moment where a love hangs in the

Opposite: Singer and actress Courtney Love, 1996. Fans and critics alike speculated that the song "Stacked Actors" was about her.

balance, and perhaps even the memory of their happiest time can't hold a couple together. There's Grohl, sappy romantic, true believer; he knows he's fighting against all odds, just like he knows there's nothing else he can do. Doomed, maybe; heroic, definitely.

Elsewhere, Grohl and his Foo Fighters favored melody over all else, his band's fearsome muscle put in deft service of expertly crafted songs, from the extended S&M metaphor in the combustive pop of "Gimme Stitches," the Beatles-like strum of "Next Year" (the final single released from the album, and later used as theme tune for NBC's quirky dramedy *Ed*) to the taut "Headwires," which, with its chorus-slaked guitar parts, seemed to indulge Hawkins's love for The Police. Penned and recorded during mixing sessions for the album, "Live-In Skin" is no afterthought, an elemental triumph built on an oscillating riff that came to Grohl unexpectedly, after he thought the album was complete. The LP's final two tracks, meanwhile, both possessed a cinematic, as-the-end-credits-roll quality, with Grohl's porch-song "Ain't It The Life" sound-tracking another lazily beautiful sunset in Alexandria, followed by the climactic slow-burn of "M.I.A."—a love song that also dramatizes Grohl's dropping out of the LA rock scene, his return to Virginia, and his gleeful slipping off of the grid. "I'm leaving, going M.I.A.,"

he howls, but he knows he won't be alone, adding, "Getting lost in you again is better than being numb."

There were still traces of Foo Fighters' punk roots on the album, though they were mostly consigned to the opening pair of rockers. The second track, "Breakout" was an exhilarating, almost self-parodyingly numbskull mosh-a-long, and written around an extended acne-related metaphor. Opener, "Stacked Actors" meanwhile, was no joke. Grohl had penned the riff before the sessions began, perhaps explaining why its metallic thrash seems so out of step with the rest of the album, for a mooted project with heavy metal godhead Ozzy Osbourne, but the Sabbath man rejected it. "I was trying to come up with riffs that I thought would sound cool—Ozzy circa his *Crazy Train* era—and I was just fooling around when I tuned the E down to A. But I loved how sludge-heavy the guitar sounded, and I decided to keep the riffs for myself," Grohl told *Guitar Player*.

It was Ozzy's loss, as Grohl cranked that riff—and its quiet-to-loud swing from loungey sleaze to crushing, twisted-iron stomp—to eleven, his down-tuned guitar strings delivering an attack that was bruising, muscular, and wonderfully thrilling. The lyric, meanwhile, strafed the dead-eyed parade on Sunset Strip, taking aim at everything Grohl hated about Los Angeles. "It's a response to living in Hollywood for a year and a half," Grohl told *Sway* magazine, "and my disdain and disgust for everything plastic and phony, which is the foundation of that city. And I just hated it. I had a lot of fun, but I had a lot of fun hating it."

Many critics interpreted the lyrics as aimed at Kurt's widow, Courtney Love, who had revived her acting career with her Golden Globe-nominated performance in Miloš Forman's 1996 movie, *The People vs. Larry Flynt*, and scored some commercial success with Hole's third album, 1998's *Celebrity Skin*. Though Grohl always tried to keep a lid on it in his interviews, it was assumed by many that Grohl and Love shared a fractious relationship, aggravated by her role as the

"The most important thing about writing songs is to refuse the specifics, because that takes away the opportunity for some listener to relate to the song. I wrote 'Stacked Actors' about everything that is fake and everything that is plastic and unreal, so if that pertains to anyone that comes to mind, then there you go."

DAVE GROHL

Taylor Hawkins, Dave Grohl and Chris Shiflett, 1999

> "I joined the band, and we bonded on tour a week later. I was just wide-eyed— I jumped in with both feet."
>
> **CHRIS SHIFLETT**

executor of Kurt's estate, and therefore the person with the last word on Nirvana's posthumous output. With its hook of "We cry when they all die blond," interviewers dwelt upon who on earth the subject of "Stacked Actors" might be, while Grohl tried gentle-manfully to deflect, telling *NME*, "I've been asked that question about every song I've written. The most important thing about writing songs is to refuse the specifics, because that takes away the opportunity for some listener to relate to the song. I wrote 'Stacked Actors' about everything that is fake and everything that is plastic and unreal, so if that pertains to anyone that comes to mind, then there you go."

With the album completed, there were business matters at hand. The previous summer, Capitol Records' former president Gary Gersh left the company, leading Grohl to act on the "Key Man" clause in Foo Fighters' contract with the label. The group had been unsigned throughout the sessions for *There Is Nothing Left to Lose*, lending a further meaning to the title, a sentiment of optimism from the darkness, lifted from the lyrics to "Generator."

Being without a record label was, Grohl told *Billboard*, a liberating experience. "It was intoxicating—we were left to our own devices. The album was purely our creation, not open to outside tampering." Once completed, Grohl shopped the album around the record labels, to find Foo Fighters a new home. He ended up signing with RCA, America's second-oldest record label and one-time home to Elvis Presley. "This is the most comfortable the band has ever come across on record," boasted RCA's vice president of marketing, David Gottlieb. "It's no longer the guy from Nirvana who started a band after Kurt Cobain died. Dave Grohl has developed into a strong artistic presence of his own."

While *There's Nothing Left to Lose* proved that, as a stripped-down trio, Foo Fighters could still make some of the greatest music of their young career, Grohl realized he couldn't play all the guitar parts live on his own, and that the group needed another guitarist. But while he'd previously assembled the Foo Fighters' line-up by tapping friends and people that he knew, Grohl chose instead to hold an open audition for the spot, realizing, he said, "how important it is that we find someone that really works personally and musically." Given the turnover

Right: New Foo Fighters guitarist Chris Shiflett bonds with his bandmates—and Tenacious D's Jack Black and Kyle Gass—in LA.

Learn To Fly

of Foo Fighters members in such a short period of time, one can forgive Grohl for thinking a change was as good as a rest.

The auditions were long and exhaustive, with no less than forty musicians showing up to demonstrate their skills, as the Foos took over Mates rehearsal studio in North Hollywood for a week or two. The winning candidate would arrive late in the audition process. A veteran of the Santa Barbara punk rock scene, Chris Shiflett had played in a slew of groups, from his hardcore band Rat Pack to high-profile pop-punk outfits like No Use for a Name and Me First and the Gimme Gimmes. "I remember thinking, 'Dave's much taller than I'd thought he'd be,'" Shiflett told me of the audition. "I walked into the room and just thought, 'Wow! He's big. . .'"

Shiflett blitzed the audition, but there was more to the job of being a Foo Fighter than just playing your instrument—what was he like as a dude, as someone the others would be sharing touring life with for days on end? Grohl was encouraged when he realized he'd met Shiflett years before, when Rat Pack had supported Scream at a gig in Santa Barbara in the eighties. "The fact that he was a part of that underground punk rock thing was really important to me," Grohl told the director of *Foo Fighters: Back and Forth,* James Moll. "He's gonna understand, and he won't take this shit for granted."

Shiflett spent the day after the audition on tenterhooks, until Grohl called to say he'd got the job, and to turn up early for rehearsal the next day, as they had a year's worth of touring already booked. "I joined the band, and we bonded on tour a week later," Shiflett remembers. "I was just wide-eyed—I jumped in with both feet."

Making fast friends with his new bandmates, Shiflett proved Grohl's instincts correct—or at least some of them, anyway. "I thought he was this mellow, soft-spoken guy," Grohl told me. "And once he joined the band, he turned into one of the biggest partiers I've ever seen in my life. I remember when he started out, thinking, 'My god, are you that same guy who tried out with us three and a half weeks ago? Hey! Wow!'"

Shiflett would soon get to satisfy his taste for on-the-road partying. The group played a secret show at Hollywood's Troubadour club on September 3, billed as "Stacked Actors." Their first concert of 1999 and Shiflett's concert debut as a Foo Fighter, it lit the touchpaper for two years of intense touring, racking up 194 further performances before the wheels well and truly fell off the wagon. In addition to the heavy concert schedule, the touring for *There Is Nothing Left to Lose* brought with it new pressures, with the Foos joining the Red Hot Chili Peppers for a four-month North American trek of stadiums and similar enormodomes. The Foos took the challenge of these vast open spaces seriously, concentrating on developing a whip-smart live show that could deliver on such a grand scale, and work visually as well as sonically. No more would the Foos turn up in t-shirts and jeans, instead dressing only in black, red, and white, Dave clothed in black shirt and white tie, Nate dressed all in red and, most nights, Taylor stripped to his waist by several songs. They even built a stage set centered around an artillery of colored lights, in sly tribute to the sleeve of their beloved Queen's landmark 1979 concert album *Live Killers*. "We put on this show, and we fucking killed it," Grohl later told Moll.

The pressure of the touring was further exacerbated by Grohl's agreeing to lots of promo work while on the road, and during the week of downtime every month the Chilis' touring schedule allowed. Interviews, TV appearances, radio appearances all ate up the breathing space between shows and travel, and while the Foos' stamina remained impressive, a

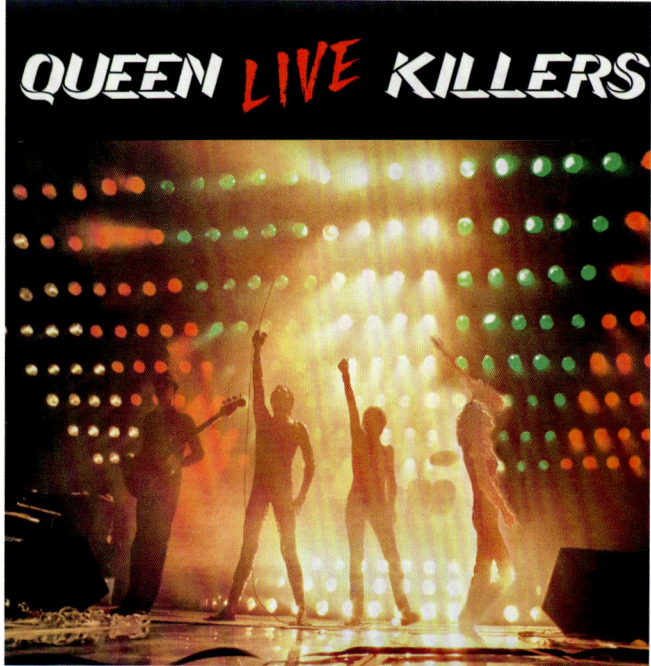

Left: Foo Fighters' stellar new lighting rig was influenced by the sleeve of Queen's *Live Killers* LP.

year in Grohl was already beginning to register the wear and tear, telling *Melody Maker* in September 2000 that he'd just discovered, at the age of thirty-one, his first couple of grey hairs. "I blame it on our touring schedule," he said. "People asked me, 'When did your father go grey?', and I said, 'He didn't go grey until he was about fifty.' Then I'm like 'Oh my god! I'm killing myself on the road!'"

Luckily, the success of *There Is Nothing Left to Lose* helped keep the Foos' spirits buoyant during their months of hard labor. The album reached the Top 10 in the US and the UK and scored well across the globe, while "Learn To Fly" proved a platinum-selling single, sent aloft by another popular Jesse Peretz promo video that plastered MTV wall-to-wall with the Foos' hilarious, *Airplane*-esque in-flight madness. Guest-starring Jack Black and Kyle Gass, the video featured Taylor in drag as a flight attendant, and Dave, in pigtails and braces, as a Foo Fighters fan who can't believe her hero is on the same flight.

The reviews were solid, *Rolling Stone*'s three-and-a-half-star rave commending Grohl's "greater emphasis on melody and actual singing", while *Entertainment Weekly*'s B-plus grade reflected "a sensitive streak that meshes nicely with Grohl's more aggressive inclinations." And while the *L.A. Times* bemoaned that *There Is Nothing Left to Lose* "fails to soar beyond the usual cache of worthwhile tracks already destined for endless airplay on modern rock radio," the Recording Academy awarded it the Grammy Award for the Best Rock Album—the group's first Grammy—along with the gong for Best Short Form Music Video for "Learn To Fly."

It was sweet vindication for Grohl, who had signaled his commitment to the band by getting the Foo Fighters' "FF" logo tattooed on his neck for the sleeve photo to *There Is Nothing Left to Lose*. But as the grind of the tour began to bite, his thoughts turned elsewhere, to musical ideas and ambitions which perhaps didn't fit within the parameters sketched out so far by the Foo Fighters. "A lot of the music I find most beautiful or pleasurable is long, slow, sleepy, quiet instrumentals that have nothing to do with structure or pop convention," he told *Select* in 2000. "I have this fantasy of a nice two-month stretch off at home with no-one around but me, just to see what came out. What would it be like? The sleepiest, slowest 'Tangerine Dream' bullshit."

Just such a furlough was visited upon Grohl in the summer of 2001 when, in the midst of a batch of European festival shows, Foo Fighters found themselves on involuntary hiatus. During that enforced downtime, Grohl pursued a series of freelance projects that redrew the frontiers of his achievements and allowed him to live out some rock 'n' roll dreams. Indeed, Grohl would soon find himself having to choose between these new opportunities, and a band which had grown wildly dysfunctional as it lumbered through recording a fourth album which looked like it might serve as their epitaph.

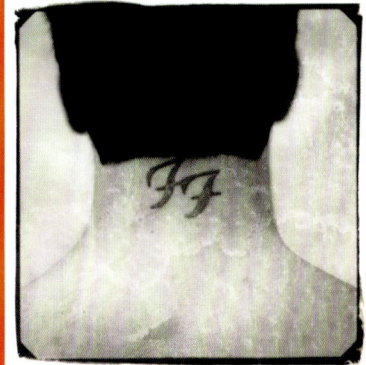

There Is Nothing Left to Lose

Released: November 2, 1999
Label: Roswell/RCA
Recorded: March–June, 1999
Studio 606, Alexandria, Virginia
Conway Recording Studios, Los Angeles, California

PERSONNEL:
Dave Grohl: lead vocals, guitars, drums, percussion, loops, Mellotron on "Next Year"
Nate Mendel: bass
Taylor Hawkins: drums, percussion

Additional personnel:
Adam Kasper: producer, recording, mixing

TRACK LISTING:
All tracks written by Dave Grohl, Nate Mendel, and Taylor Hawkins

1. "Stacked Actors"
2. "Breakout"
3. "Learn To Fly"
4. "Gimme Stitches"
5. "Generator"
6. "Aurora"
7. "Live-In Skin"
8. "Next Year"
9. "Headwires"
10. "Ain't It The Life"
11. "M.I.A."

Foo Fighters, 2002. (L-R) Nate Mendel, Taylor Hawkins, Dave Grohl, Chris Shiflett

Times Like These

"Bands shouldn't last forever, there's always an expiration date. I thought we should call it quits and end it on a high note."

DAVE GROHL

Today, California's Coachella Valley Music and Arts Festival is an event with few equals in the calendar of the global entertainment industry. Every year, over two spring weekends at the Empire Polo Club, Coachella draws together an eclectic bill of the world's more in-demand rock, pop, rap, and soul stars amid the dunes of the Colorado Desert, like Glastonbury with reliably blissful sunshine, and cactii instead of ley lines. The 2017 festival—Coachella's eighteenth, headlined by Radiohead, Lady Gaga, and Kendrick Lamar—welcomed 250,000 festival-goers and grossed $114.6million, the first time a recurring American festival banked box office of over nine figures. Its early years, however, were a slightly more modest affair.

The festival had begun in 1999, a two-day event in October headlined by Beck, Rage Against the Machine, and Tool, but drew barely more than half of its projected seventy thousand attendees, leaving promoters Goldenvoice $850,000 in the hole, and unsure of their future. To keep Coachella afloat, a number of the artists—including all the headliners—agreed to defer their fees for the festival. Coachella returned in April 2001 as a one-day festival, with its star attraction the reunion of the legendarily combustive Jane's Addiction, fronted by the flamboyant Perry Farrell, the Lollapalooza-founding ringleader of a generation who'd coined the concept of the "Alternative Nation." The 2001 festival lost markedly less money than the first Coachella, so Goldenvoice plowed on.

The third Coachella Festival took place the weekend of April 27-28, 2002, and boasted another commendably varied program of entertainment, with Björk and Oasis headlining, and hotly tipped new indie-rock groups like The Vines and The Strokes duking it out with the likes of KRS-ONE, Siouxsie and the Banshees, and The Prodigy across four stages.

Third-down on the bill on the main Coachella stage, Sunday night, were the Foo Fighters, playing only their fourth concert of the year.

Everyone expected it to be a momentous show, not least as the group had published a press release a week or so before Coachella signaling that the festival performance would precede a hiatus for

Opposite: Foo Fighters, 2002, Chicago, USA. The band spent much of this period aboard a tour bus.

Right: Taylor Hawkins. His heavy partying left him in a coma in a London hospital following a heroin overdose.

"Seeing Dave play with Queens would have been like going to see your girlfriend fuck some other dude."

TAYLOR HAWKINS

the group. But only those who'd been hanging out with the Foo Fighters backstage the last couple of days, truly knew how close their performance that weekend came to being their last.

The band had been mostly on ice for a number of months, during which time Dave Grohl accepted an offer from desert-rock hellions Queens of the Stone Age to drum on their third album, *Songs for the Deaf*. Grohl was pulling double duty at Coachella that weekend, drumming with Queens on Saturday evening.

Grohl's extra-curricular activity caused tension within the ranks, especially as his Queens commitments had coincided with stalled sessions for a fourth Foo Fighters LP, stirring anxiety within the group over their future. Grohl was bummed that Hawkins, his brother from another mother and kindred drumming spirit, hadn't come to see him play with Queens when they'd performed their now-legendary first show with Grohl at LA's Troubadour. Hawkins, dealing with his own issues—more on which later—was in turn angry that Grohl couldn't see that he was too busy with his own struggles to cheer Grohl on as he "cheated" on his day job. "Seeing Dave play with Queens would have been like going to see your girlfriend fuck some other dude," Hawkins told *MOJO*.

Like all good boys, they didn't have it out immediately, preferring to stew as they began rehearsals for Sunday's show. After a period of stultifying, uncomfortable rehearsal—perhaps spurred on by a sense that this dream job he had only recently caught might already be over, and before he'd had a chance to make a record with them—Chris Shiflett broke the stalemate, quipping, "Is it just me or could you cut the air in here with a fuckin' knife? What the fuck's going on?"

All hell broke loose. Soon, everyone was shouting, the fight fiercest between Grohl and Hawkins. "I'll be leaving, once we've played Coachella and finished the album, once my commitments are done," yelled Hawkins. "I'm out of here."

Hitting an emotional wall, Grohl wearily replied, "Let's just do this show. And if we never want to do this again, let's never do this again."

If the big crisis hit in the summer of 2001, the rot was setting in long before that. The touring for *There Is Nothing Left to Lose* was heavy, and wore hard and deep on the Foo Fighters, who kept their spirits up by keeping spirits down. First, it was a shot before the show. Then, it was ten shots. Then it was getting so loose that holding it together for the course of the show became a challenge worth accepting—anything to shake the numbing, Groundhog Day psychosis of day after day on the road. "That's probably why so many musicians get so fucked up," Shiflett mused to filmmaker James Moll. "You need something to keep it fun."

Taylor Hawkins was keeping things very "fun" indeed. "I was partying a lot," he later recalled. "I wasn't, like, a junkie, per se, but I was partying a lot. I was the dumb kid that was just taking it too far. If you put a line of something in front of me, I was, like, 'Yeah, I'll do that.' There was a year where the partying just got a little too heavy. This guy gave me the wrong line or the wrong thing one night. . .and that was a real changing point for me."

That pivotal moment happened in England, where the group were kicking off a spate of festival dates across Europe with the V Festival, playing consecutive nights at the event's two sites in Stafford and Chelmsford. It was while partying backstage after their set at Chelmsford that Hawkins encountered that "wrong line," leaving him in a coma in a London hospital, following a heroin overdose.

Upon learning of Hawkins's misadventure, Grohl raced to his bedside, where he remained for a fortnight, waiting for

Left: Grohl's appearance with Queens of the Stone Age at the 2002 Coachella music festival left his bandmates wondering if Foo Fighters were done.

Right: Chris Shiflett Coachella 2002, Empire Polo Field, Indio, California, USA

Hawkins to come round. Those weeks, he later told *MOJO*'s Paul Brannigan, were "the first time in my life that I ever considered quitting music. Because I was wondering if music just equaled death. I didn't want to do music if everyone is just gonna die all the time. I would walk from that hospital back to my hotel every night and talk to god, out loud, as I was walking. I'm not a religious person, but I was out of my mind, I was so frightened and heart-broken and confused. And I said to everyone, 'I don't even wanna hear the word Foo Fighters until I'm ready to say it again.'"

After a fortnight, Taylor came out of his coma to find Grohl at his bedside. Once his friend had his bearings again, Grohl told him they weren't going to talk about the band until Hawkins was ready. And they didn't, for a while. But while Foo Fighters slumbered, Grohl was restless. And when the invitation came to warm the drum stool of the smartest, most dangerous, and possibly most brilliant rock band of their era, well, what *was* a boy to do?

Queens of the Stone Age was the brainchild of Josh Homme, a towering, strawberry-blonde hard-man from the Californian desert who began his career with inspirational stoner-rock godheads Kyuss, then signed on as sideman for Seattle legends Screaming Trees as they embarked upon their troubled final tours, before resurfacing out amid the cacti with a new band—Queens of the Stone Age. Their 1998 eponymous debut album was a magical thing, clearly the work of underground genii, with its Stooges-meet-Krautrock chug, its eerie pop sensibility, and its gift for tempering occasional Cro-Magnon explosions of steroidal, druggy riffage with androgynous vocals and a resolute rejection of the genre's macho cliches.

Right: Queens of the Stone Age's third album, *Songs for the Deaf*, featured Grohl on drums. It's widely proclaimed as a masterpiece.

Left: Queens of the Stone Age, 2002. (L-R) Dave Grohl, Troy Van Leeuwen, Nick Oliveri, Josh Homme, and Mark Lanegan

The self-titled debut charmed a certain underground cognoscenti. But Homme's heavies unleashed the bond of cultdom with their second album, 2000's *Rated R*, a work of wired and paranoid autobiography that opened with a shopping list of intoxicants and welcomed aboard a rolling cast of ne'er-do-wells and legends, including brooding and soulful ex-Screaming Trees singer Mark Lanegan, Rob Halford of Judas Priest, and Scream's Peter Stahl. It was *Rated R*, and the touring that followed, that cemented Queens of the Stone Age's image as drug-guzzling hellraisers and angry pillagers of the heavy landscape, making them the coolest thing in rock in the process. Homme likened the group to a ship full of pirates, telling me, "on a pirate-ship, every man's important. But I'm at the helm."

"I was wondering if music just equaled death. I didn't want to do music if everyone is just gonna die all the time. I would walk from that hospital back to my hotel every night and talk to god, out loud, as I was walking. I'm not a religious person, but I was out of my mind, I was so frightened and heart-broken and confused."

DAVE GROHL

Foo Fighters: The Band That Dave Made

Homme might have been wild but, when he had to, he ran his ship with an eagle-eye and little forgiveness for slacking off. Deciding, after several weeks of sessions, that the band's then-current drummer Gene Trautmann wasn't up to the challenge of the group's forthcoming third album, Homme placed a call to Grohl to take up the drum stool for the remainder of the recording process. The previous year, Grohl—who later praised Queens of the Stone Age as "making music that's the perfect place between getting your ass kicked and being asleep"—had been asked during a radio interview what had been his biggest disappointment of 2000; he answered, "Not being asked to appear on the Queens of the Stone Age record." Now offered a chance to make good on that disappointment, Grohl grabbed the offer with two hands that hadn't really held a drumstick in a long time. "I called him about noon," Homme later remembered, "And he said he'd be there by 6.30pm. By 8pm, we had already tracked a few songs."

"People seem to consider me a legendary drummer," Grohl confessed to *Kerrang!*'s Ian Winwood. "Let me tell you, I am not a great drummer, not by a long way. And so the gig with Queens was the most pressure I've felt in a long time. It was like I was playing in a great rock band with the weight of having been the drummer in another great band weighing on my shoulders."

Be that as it may, Grohl's performances on that third Queens album, *Songs for the Deaf*, showed his modesty over his drum skills to be simply that. A swaggeringly ambitious but impressively accessible concept piece, the album played to Homme's eclectic strengths: presented as an hour's journey from Los Angeles to their desert digs, the album spun the FM dial on the car stereo and imagined the unheard classics they might find on these strange radio-waves. Homme's muse ran wild, from the brutal flamenco-metal of the doomy "First It Giveth," to the blitzing riffarama of "A Song For The Dead," to the roiling blues of Lanegan's infernal "Hangin' Tree," to the stomping sixties garage-rock of "Another Love Song." The slew of tracks mapped out an alternate rock history from another dimension, though you didn't have to squint too hard to know that, despite the sophisticated web of influences and genres on the album, it was entirely the work of Queens of the Stone Age.

Songs for the Deaf was a masterpiece, a tribute to Homme's kaleidoscopic vision, and a feel for arrangement that pared

Left: Taylor Hawkins giving it his all at 2002's Coachella music festival, Empire Polo Field, Indio, California, USA.

away any unnecessary elements and made what was left only the more powerful, that kept the excess in the dressing room and not on the tape. But it was also a tribute to Dave Grohl, unassumingly legendary drummer, his playing in perfect simpatico with Homme's less-is-more approach. Listen to the minimal fills, exploding like firecrackers through "A Song For The Dead," and the way he drives the song's demon pelt and decides when its fiendish false endings will drop. Listen to how his rolling snare directs the high-drama of "First It Giveth," or lends "No One Knows" its taut funk and tumbledown explosions, or sends the midnight tornado of "Hangin' Tree" senselessly spinning. His mighty economy as a drummer was a crucial element of the album, and he was hugely proud of it, telling all who would listen that *Songs for the Deaf* was going to "change the face of music."

You can only imagine how Nate, or Chris, or (most of all) Taylor felt when they heard that. Their feelings were especially raw, as the Foos had been suspended at a most unfulfilled point. Earlier in 2001, the group had gathered at Taylor Hawkins's home in LA's legendary old hippie hangout Topanga Canyon, to demo songs they'd written on tour for the proposed fourth Foo Fighters album. Those sessions were then paused as the group set off for the ill-fated European festival tour, the one quickly canceled following Hawkins's overdose.

The Foos reconvened in October, to finish work on the new songs, before decamping to Grohl's home studio in Alexandria to begin recording the album. But a couple of months in the basement yielded only six finished tracks before the band hit a wall and succumbed to collective ennui. Taylor was still dealing with the aftermath of his overdose and negotiating his way towards a more sober lifestyle. Nate was arguing with Grohl over arrangements and songs. Grohl felt everyone's playing was half-assed. Shiflett was wondering if his new band would survive their first album with him.

"The vibes," Grohl later said, "were not happening." A move of operations to Los Angeles, and the secluded Conway Studios, barely perked up the band. They seemed to be grouchily sleepwalking through the new album.

Grohl's rehearsals for Queens of the Stone Age's upcoming show at the Troubadour, debuting *Songs for the Deaf*, and marking Grohl's first public performance with the Queens, threw the differences between the two bands into sharp relief. Where work on the new Foo Fighters album had devolved into wading through truculent molasses, those Queens rehearsals were electric, Grohl sensing he was in the company of a band about to hit a creative and commercial peak. "At night I'd go and rehearse in a closet with Queens and be totally energized," he told Paul Brannigan, "and then come to Conway and be totally dismayed by the apathy." An interviewer and photographer from *Kerrang!* had dropped by the studio during the Conway sessions and narrowly missed an argument between Grohl and his bandmates that boiled over, with Grohl threatening to break up the band then and there.

They held together, and completed an album's worth of material. But when it came time to submit it to the label, Grohl listened back to what they recorded and felt little enthusiasm. Upon receipt of the finished album, manager John Silva said dismissively, "Well, we can put this out. But I can't guarantee we'll be able to sell any of them."

Tormented by the substandard music he'd just finished recording, Grohl came to a decision. In March, following Queen of the Stone Age's triumphant Troubadour show, he told the rest of the Foos that they were scrapping the album, that he'd told the label they'd be reworking it and delivering it later, and that he was going to drum with Queens that summer. The music they'd been recording didn't feel right, but playing with Queens did. He imagined having to do press for the new album as it currently was, having to say he was proud of it, and knew he'd be lying if he said so.

As Coachella fast approached, Grohl posted a message to the fans on the Foo Fighters' own website that signaled he was kicking a fourth album into the long grass for a while. "After four months, three studios and who knows how many foosball tables, we decided to take a break from it," he wrote. "We thought it might be a good idea to sit back and chill out a little bit. I mean, I can't wait to release this stuff, it's really kick-ass, but I think we're going to relax, and record some more."

This missive painted an unconvincing smiley face upon the rest of the Foos' dismay over the uncertainty of the group's future. Taylor, of course, took it hardest. Homebreaker Homme himself reflected, "Band people are very easily rattled. I always knew Dave was going to go back to the Foo Fighters; I was always trying to intimate that this wasn't something the other guys needed to worry about, but that's kinda impossible, because sometimes people can hear those words and think they're being stitched up."

Truly, Hawkins had gotten the feeling he was being cheated. "I know he wasn't trying to hurt me," he later said, of Grohl's actions then. "But our band was falling apart. It was a tough time, and it felt a little hurtful to me, too. Because it spelled out the end of our band."

Opposite: Foo Fighters, 2002, Chicago, USA. (L-R) Nate Mendel, Taylor Hawkins, Dave Grohl, Chris Shiflett

> "Band people are very easily rattled. I always knew Dave was going to go back to the Foo Fighters; I was always trying to intimate that this wasn't something the other guys needed to worry about, but that's kinda impossible, because sometimes people can hear those words and think they're being stitched up."
>
> **JOSH HOMME**

This oncoming storm of resentment, guilt, and frustration churned within the group, until the argument during the Coachella rehearsals caused the clouds to break. Faced with Foo Fighters' current sleepwalk into oblivion, Grohl realized he had to take charge and right his own ship, perhaps inspired by Homme's Blackbeard ways. Before they walked onto the Coachella stage that night, Hawkins's threat to quit the group still ringing in his ears, Grohl took charge and made clear that this could be their final show, if they wanted it to be.

"I thought, 'Well, that was fun and we've had a good run,'" Grohl remembered later. "Bands shouldn't last forever, there's always an expiration date. I thought we should call it quits and end it on a high note."

"It actually helped clear the air and save the band," remarked Hawkins, later, of Grohl's putting the fate of the Foo Fighters up in the air. "That was when Dave let everyone know, 'I'm leading this band.' It was, 'Don't question me—everyone can have their opinion, but I'm the leader, I'm gonna have the final word, I'm gonna make the decisions and I'm gonna essentially write the songs.' And everyone went, 'OK, well, now I understand where we're at.' The dynamic changed a bit, but in a way it made things easier."

Certainly, the tensions that fueled their rehearsal room conflict translated into what many consider one of the Foos' most electric sets ever, that evening at Coachella. Gone were the big stage sets and the color-coordinated wardrobes—Grohl dressed down in white tee and chinos, goateed and mustached, riffing away at his Lucite guitar, Shiflett bruising his Flying-V in denims—but the impact was bigger than any of their recent stadium shows. That night, as the sun set behind the palm trees that framed the stage, the Foo Fighters were a band fighting for their lives, playing more furiously and ferociously than ever before, like it was their last stand—which, as far as anyone onstage knew, it probably was.

On the cusp of what appeared to be the end, the Foos still looked to some kind of a future, debuting a new song, "All My Life," its bullet-pointed riffage seemingly echoing the flab-free muscularity of *Songs for the Deaf*, and swerving hard from the gauzy classic rock of *There Is Nothing Left to Lose*, in a much harder direction. "The last album was loose and melodic, almost as a response or a reaction to the aggressive and tight metal that was all over the place at the time," Grohl had told *Kerrang!* during the Conway sessions, promising, "On this record, I think you'll hear more energy."

Ultimately, Grohl had decided that their most recent recordings lacked that energy. It was abundantly present onstage at Coachella that Sunday evening, however. Grohl shone that night, stooped menacingly over his microphone, bellowing and howling away. "Dave was like a new frontman," marveled Shiflett, later. And the Foo Fighters seemed a renewed band. All of them agreed after the show that the performance had been a watershed, that whatever chemistry had taken them this far was still there, still worth salvaging. Grohl was about to head off with Queens of the Stone Age, but there was a two-week window in his schedule, between legs of the Queens tour. He told the boys to join him in Virginia, and they'd jam some.

En route, Grohl visited Hawkins in his Topanga abode, and the two of them demoed a couple more new songs, just instrumentals at this point, but songs which would underpin the album that followed, "Low" and "Times Like These."

Opposite: Josh Homme of Queens of the Stone Age. He understood Grohl's tenure with his group would unsettle the Foo Fighters.

Grohl would work the latter tune into a fiery anthem that was also frankly autobiographical; simply, the song was the "Ballad of the Foo Fighters," or at least this last year of their existence. "It was basically written about the band disappearing for those two or three months," he later explained, "and me feeling like I wasn't entirely myself."

From Topanga the duo flew to Alexandria where, in seven days, they rerecorded the album at Studio 606, retracking the drums, the vocals, and many of the guitar parts. "It just came together," Grohl told *Spin*. "There was no time to fuck around, no time to over-analyze, it was just all about making music because we were excited to do it and the energy was there."

That energy translated into some of the heaviest music the Foos had so far recorded. And those seven days in Virginia had achieved something months in a big budget recording studio had failed at: producing an album Foo Fighters would be willing to release. The irony was not lost on Grohl, who compared the Conway version of opener "All My Life" with the version recorded at Studio 606 as an illustration; the former, he said, "Cost a million dollars and sounded like crap." The version they recorded in his basement in half an hour, meanwhile, went on to become "the biggest fuckin' song the band ever had."

Grohl spent most of that summer, however, as drummer with Queens of the Stone Age, an experience he relished. "It was the first time I've ever felt truly confident and strong in a band," he later reflected to *Hot Press*, of joining the last heavy rock gang in town. "Walking backstage at a festival with Queens is like the moment in a Western where the saloon bar doors swing open and the piano player stops playing and everyone just stares. We didn't have to talk about anything, it was just so fuckin' easy: every night we went onstage I knew that we were the best band on the bill, because it felt that way."

The challenge, of course, was bringing this energy back to the Foo Fighters. But at least the backstage confrontation during the run-up to Coachella had shown him that he was willing to fight for the Foo Fighters' future. He retired from the Queens of the Stone Age drum stool after their show at the Fuji Rock Festival in Japan on Sunday, July 28, though he'd return later. After all, Homme said, Queens was Grohl's "mistress." But for now, Grohl realized that "the Foo Fighters had become a family, and I'd been away from home for too long."

That year had seen Dave Grohl revisit his heavy-rockin', hardcore punk roots, in reaction to the softer pleasures he'd explored on the Foo Fighters' previous album. The disparate members of Queens of the Stone Age had bonded, he'd said, over their shared love for Californian hardcore pioneers Black Flag, to the point where Grohl was even writing drum parts in tribute to legendary drummer Bill Stevenson. The Foo Fighters, meanwhile, had just recorded an album that chased away the string sections and pedal steels with which Grohl had latterly been toying, using flinty, distorted guitars to scrub away their memory.

Opposite: Coachella, 2002. Grohl's bandmates agreed that he'd never before assumed the role of frontman with such vigor.

Touring the soft-rock confections of the previous album had awoken the ire of the boy who had discovered rock via the brutish brilliance of AC/DC. Months of playing "Learn To Fly" had stripped it of meaning for Grohl, giving him an itch to ricochet in the opposite sonic direction. Desperate to show himself he could "do something else other than AM-radio 'alternative' McDonald's pop," he'd penned a batch of new tunes that took a different tack, that didn't even sound like Foo Fighters songs.

Their fourth album, *One by One* would easily prove their heaviest and most metallic yet. But while there was nary a talk box present across its eleven tracks, the burgeoning melodic maturity displayed on *There Is Nothing Left to Lose* still pulsed within the songs, leavening its harshest moments and lurking within the melee. "Lonely As You's" heavy, detuned guitars made like a string section, echoing the similar trick played by Soundgarden on their 1994 classic "The Day I Tried To Live," and sounding like ELO cloaked in grungy trappings. The dirgey soft-pop balladry of "Tired" played a similar trick, its Badfinger bleakness delineated by guitars multi-tracked into a symphonic threnody, courtesy of Brian May, guitarist with Queen, and one of a number of high-profile rock legends Grohl had latterly befriended.

Elsewhere, Grohl's gift for pop songwriting rose to the challenge of the new album's more violent feel for dynamics; the TV commercial jingle "I'd Like To Buy The World A Coke" was reborn as headrush rock 'n' roll on "Overdrive," while "Have It All" proved that even in this more savage new incarnation, Grohl hadn't discarded the lessons he'd learned in songcraft, its hairpin turns and rampant heaviness underscored by sweet soft rock. And the bombastic, drum-heavy stomp of "Burn Away" was nevertheless touched with the romance and poetry of prime Thin Lizzy, Grohl's nagging chorus of "Burn away, burn away, burn away my bride" just begging for some heroic twin-lead guitar solos from Scott Gorham and Brian Robertson.

But *One by One*'s character was defined by its bridge-burning first track "All My Life," its tense opening, Grohl's rhythm guitar ticking like a time-bomb, swiftly flaring into feedback, before swerving into a riff that's like being slammed into a wall, and then slammed into a wall again, and then slammed into that wall a few more times, and enjoying it. Grohl later quipped that the lyrics were "a little dirty." Certainly, if *There Is Nothing Left*

Foo Fighters: The Band That Dave Made

to Lose was an album about the search for self and true love, "All My Life" aimed several inches lower, a tale of libido as a priapic state, with Grohl howling, "I'm done, done, then I'm onto the next one," driven senseless by his hunger, but sounding further from satisfaction than ever.

Built upon fusillades of metallic guitar that blitzed with tightly controlled violence, "Low" was another story of dysfunction, two lovers caught in a self-destructive, erotically overcharged relationship, sharing the tailspin of their lives with little regret, lost in obsession. Grohl successfully pushed to have the resolutely radio-unfriendly "Low" released as a single, precisely "because it's the coolest song on the record, but there's no way it could be a single because it's too weird." Grohl compounded "Low's" weirdness by pairing it with a music video that starred Grohl and actor Jack Black as hillbillies who rent a hotel room and get blitzed on beer, bourbon, and vodka, before arm-wrestling, dressing up in women's lingerie, trashing their room and ending the evening throwing up in the bathroom. Black, who'd also

Above: Dave Grohl with comedian Jack Black in 2002. Grohl contributed drums and guitar on all four studio albums by Black's rock band, Tenacious D.

Right: As Foo Fighters ascended into rock aristocracy, Grohl made some legendary new friends, including Queen guitarist Brian May.

guest-starred in the video for "Learn To Fly," was another of Grohl's celebrity friends; Grohl had drummed on the platinum-selling eponymous debut by Tenacious D, the comedy rock band Black fronted with collaborator Kyle Gass, a year earlier.

These tales of hedonistic abandon mapped out new lyrical territory for Grohl, a walk on a darker, wilder side. But the greatest song on *One by One*—indeed, in Grohl's own estimation, "the best song I've ever written"—"Times Like These" returns to the themes of struggle and redemption that are Grohl's typical stomping grounds. As mentioned above, for Grohl the song represented his own sense of loss and confusion during the days when it looked like Foo Fighters were done, and, over brash, post-punk, high-impact guitar chords, he revisited that feeling of having the ground fall out beneath him, asking, "Do I stay or run away. And leave it all behind?" But again, Grohl's belief in some kind of redemption wins out, those chords on the chorus surer and firmer, as he reasons that such depths of despair are the making of you. Making the personal universal was a skill very much within Grohl's wheelhouse, as was penning music that inspired without ever descending into schlock.

> "There's a lot more to being in a band than just being in a band. It's like a marriage, an unspoken foundation, and it's something you know you rely on. Just knowing it's there in the back of your mind sort of props you up and keeps you going."
>
> **DAVE GROHL**

Opposite: Foo Fighters (L-R) Chris Shiflett, Dave Grohl, Taylor Hawkins, Nate Mendel, Brussels, Belgium, November 2002

Played out most explicitly on "Times Like These," redemption was a theme Grohl would return to again and again. And why not? Everything in Dave Grohl's biography suggested that despair wasn't the end, at least not for him—that tears will dry, that American lives could have second acts, that even when your band look like they're completely on the outs, they can still walk into the basement of a humble home in a Virginia suburb and crack out their most successful hit in under half an hour. And that the band could have their meanest, harshest fight, and come out of it stronger, happier and more well-adjusted than ever.

"There's a lot more to being in a band than just being in a band," Grohl later explained to *Kerrang!* "It's like a marriage, an unspoken foundation, and it's something you know you rely on. Just knowing it's there in the back of your mind sort of props you up and keeps you going." Grohl had been unable to shake the temptation represented by Queens of the Stone Age, his rock 'n' roll "mistress"—"If there's any band that you can dip your toes into and then run away, it's Queens," he said—but his "marriage" with Foo Fighters had managed to survive this dalliance.

However, Grohl had now developed a taste for playing the field. And in the years that followed, it seemed that the best way to keep Foo Fighters happy was to treat the group like an open marriage, with Grohl free to work with who he pleased. This freedom would offer Grohl the opportunity to collaborate on several momentous side-projects, and it would also lead Foo Fighters towards their most ambitious album yet.

"It was a rare moment which proved that having multiple personalities isn't a bad thing for someone playing music," Josh Homme told Paul Brannigan, of Dave Grohl's extra-Foo-rricular activities. "Because once you feel you can do anything in music, that's when you can get closer to God."

One by One
Grammy Award Best Rock Album, 2004

Released: October 22, 2002
Label: Roswell / RCA
Recorded: April–May, 2002
Studio 606, Alexandria, Virginia

PERSONNEL:
Dave Grohl: lead vocals, backing vocals, rhythm guitar, lead guitar, piano on "Come Back"
Nate Mendel: bass
Taylor Hawkins: drums, percussion, lead vocals on "Life Of Illusion"
Chris Shiflett: lead guitar, rhythm guitar, lead vocals on "Danny Says"

Additional personnel:
Brian May: guitar on "Tired Of You"
Krist Novoselic: backing vocals on "Walking A Line"
Gregg Bissonette: drums on "Danny Says"
Adam Kasper: producer on "Tired Of You"
Nick Raskulinecz: engineer, producer

TRACK LISTING:
All tracks written by Dave Grohl, Taylor Hawkins, Nate Mendel, and Chris Shiflett, except where noted

1. "All My Life"
2. "Low"
3. "Have It All"
4. "Times Like These"
5. "Disenchanted Lullaby"
6. "Tired Of You"
7. "Halo"
8. "Lonely As You"
9. "Overdrive"
10. "Burn Away"
11. "Come Back"

BONUS CD EDITION
1. "Walking A Line"
2. "Sister Europe"
3. "Danny Says"
4. "Life Of Illusion"
5. "For All The Cows" (live)
6. "Monkey Wrench" (live)
7. "Next Year"

DISCOGRAPHY

Foo Fighters, 2005. (L-R) Chris Shiflett, Taylor Hawkins, Dave Grohl, Nate Mendel

Best Of You

"For once in my life I've made a record I don't want to be the last. It's opening doors I can see through for ten more years. And that's never happened before."

DAVE GROHL

One by One was only Dave Grohl's most high-profile act of penance for the soft-rock crimes he now perceived *There Is Nothing Left to Lose* to be guilty of. In that same bout of downtime when he penned the songs that sounded "nothing like Foo Fighters" but would go on to compose their fourth album, Grohl came up with a further bunch of riffs which all sounded even less like Foo Fighters songs.

The smash success of "Learn To Fly" did not inure Grohl to the song; indeed, repeat performances of its uplifting chorus caused him to recognize it as "the most middle-of-the-road pop song I had ever written." And there's a place for middle-of-the-road pop, and as middle-of-the-road pop went, "Learn To Fly" was among the greatest. But repeat exposure to his own Boomer-friendly ballad caused conflict and cognitive dissonance for the member of Nirvana most likely to have unironically worn double-denim in his youth. "What am I doing, man?" Grohl reeled. "Some of my favorite bands in the world are completely into Satan and fucking play a thousand miles an hour. This is ridiculous."

Grohl needed to get back to the source, to get back in touch with his basest metal. He had to get back to Jimmy Swanson.

Dave Grohl has never explicitly credited Jimmy Swanson as an inspiration for "My Hero," but there's little doubt he would qualify. Swanson was, Grohl told *Q* magazine, "my partner in crime, from the time I was six or seven years old. The first time I smoked weed, he lit the bowl. The first time I went on tour, he was my roadie." Swanson lived a block away from Grohl and, as they grew up, the duo bonded over their love of hardcore punk. But Swanson also had a taste for heavier pleasures, ordering elusive early thrash classics via mail order record store End Of The Rainbow. It was Swanson who first initiated Grohl in the ways of metal. One day he received a package containing Metallica's deathless debut album, *Kill 'Em All*; ten

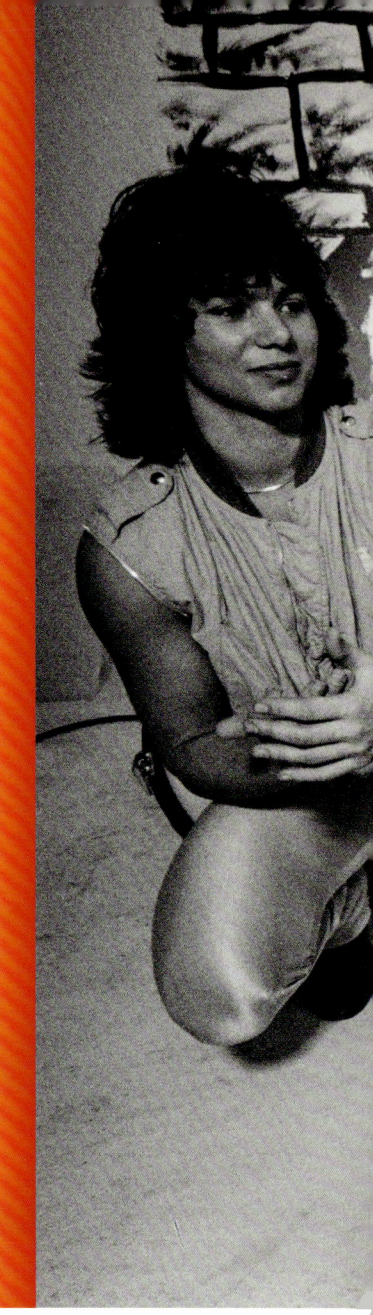

Right: Danish metallers Mercyful Fate, whose singer King Diamond (center) would guest on Grohl's metal side-project, *Probot*

Left: Metallica's debut album, *Kill 'Em All,* had been a primal, powerful influence on a juvenile Grohl.

seconds after laying the needle down, Swanson correctly surmising that this would be a life-changing record, and called Grohl to come on over.

They listened to the album in its entirety, wordless, rapt by its speed, its precision, its ferocity. "We were like, 'Oh my god!'" Swanson later remembered. "The closest thing we had heard was Motörhead, but this was, like, times ten."

The duo were now entirely switched on to heaviness, and changed their musical habits accordingly, subsisting on a diet favoring only the purest metal. The early eighties was a rich era for the genre, and Swanson introduced Grohl to the dark thrills of Illinois doom metal pioneers Trouble, face-painted Danish black-metallers Mercyful Fate, and Californian proto-thrashers Dark Angel.

Grohl and Swanson weren't the only punkers of their era huffing on the fumes of one of metal's golden ages. Hardcore and this new strain of metal shared a taste for speed and violence, and the bridge between genres was crossed by a number of hardcore groups. Maryland punks Void—regulars on the D.C. hardcore scene and signed to eminent local punk imprint Dischord, run by Minor Threat's Ian MacKaye—first crossed the streams of metal and punk with their epochal split-LP with D.C. punks Faith. Later, from Houston Texas, Dirty Rotten Imbeciles (better known as DRI) evolved from frenetic "thrashcore" to an explicit mutation of the two genres, later classified as "crossover thrash," and beating a path that would swiftly be followed by metal-curious punks like North Carolina's Corrosion of Conformity, Venice, Californian punk institution Suicidal Tendencies, and New York thrashers Nuclear Assault.

Received wisdom has it that Nirvana and the coming of grunge dealt heavy metal a deathly blow, a claim that's only within bare shouting distance of the truth. The "hair-metal" era was certainly drawn to a quick close with the release of *Nevermind*, instituting a new paradigm that left the likes of

Mötley Crüe, Quiet Riot, Poison et al. looking cheap, foolish, and, worst of all, corny amid the torn denim, lumberjack shirts, and raw emotions on display. But "hair-metal" was already being superseded within metal's own community by a slew of harder, faster, edgier, and more ambitious sub-genres: speed, thrash, black, doom, and death metal were but five of the more prevalent mutations then proving that metal was alive, well, and killing its idols in the name of the future.

Grohl would later say his unabashed love for heavy metal and rock made him feel like an outsider in the indie-rock and agit-punk paradise of Olympia, Washington. And even though Swiss metal extremists Celtic Frost were a regular tour-bus-stereo favorite among his bandmates in Nirvana, and his idols Melvins an undeniably heavy, metallic proposition, Cobain would struggle throughout his career to make peace between his love of metal's sonic power, and his repulsion towards the genre's baser, misogynist inclinations. But while *Nevermind*'s success was a phenomenon that spurred an entire subculture overground, it was actually outsold by another album released only a month before, by another underground group making a boldly conscious step towards the mainstream: Metallica's eponymous "black" album.

Selling more than sixteen million copies and dragging Metallica from the alleyways of thrash to the world's stadiums via MTV smash hit "Enter Sandman" and the power ballad "Nothing Else Matters," the "black" album was an equally transformative phenomenon as *Nevermind*, opening a path to wider success for other uncompromising riffers, and setting Metallica on track to mainstream acceptance. Like Nirvana, Metallica's success would help their friends find their way overground, and lead curious listeners towards further revelations underground.

As leader of Foo Fighters, Grohl would often find himself drawn to comment on metal's state of the art, which, as the twenty-first century dawned, was the aforementioned "nu metal" era; Grohl was often diplomatic, but also signaled his alienation from the big-shorted rock-rap epoch. He still loved metal, just not this latest flavor; as ever, his ear was trained on the underground, and the deep metal masterpieces he'd immersed himself in, in his youth. And once the sweetness of "Learn To Fly" began to cloy, it was that metal he wanted to listen to, that metal he wanted to make. So he did the only thing that made sense: he went off to touch base again with old friend Jimmy Swanson.

In truth, he'd already cooked up the vague concept behind what would become *Probot* by the time he'd begun hanging out at Swanson's place, strumming super-metallic riffs on his guitar in front of the TV. He'd got the idea after guesting as a vocalist on *Iommi*, the 2000 eponymous solo debut by Black Sabbath's infernal guitarist, Tony Iommi. Grohl had played drums and sung on the track "Goodbye Lament." The other nine tracks featured nine further celebrity vocalists, from Billy Corgan, to Serj Tankian of arch metal activists System of a Down, to Billy Idol, like a heavy version of Santana's fifteen-times Platinum all-star smash, *Supernatural*.

Like Iommi's album, each *Probot* track would showcase a different vocalist, though Grohl's project would obey very strict criteria as to who those vocalists could be; chiefly, they had to have fronted underground metal bands from the era of 1986-1990. He planned to send each of these theoretical vocalists a track to sing on; like the first Foo Fighters album, each of these tracks would be played and recorded entirely by Grohl himself.

But first he had to cook up these new songs. To Grohl, Swanson was an indomitable arbiter of metallic quality. So, Grohl took up residence in Swanson's front room, riffing on his guitar with his amplifier at his feet, while Swanson watched the TV. "When I had a riff I thought was pretty good, I'd peek over at Jimmy. If he was just watching TV, then it sucked. But if he looked over, then I knew it was a keeper."

Over time, Grohl worked these riffs into songs, and cut instrumental backing tracks for them, multi-tracking in his Alexandria studio with longtime producer friend Adam Kasper. Then he sent tapes out to his dream list of collaborators, not truly believing any of these heavy heroes would lower themselves to recording a track for a side-project by "that guy from the fucking airplane video." But they would, and they did.

Perhaps the strongest argument for *Probot*'s credibility as a metal album is the caliber of talent Grohl won over to the project. Released in 2004, but recorded over 2000-2003, *Probot* featured the very artists who effected the hardcore/metal crossover, Corrosion of Conformity's Mike Dean and DRI's Kurt Brecht, who Grohl greeted by grinning, "Hey man, it's me: I bought a single out of the back of your van twenty years ago"; the singers who first won Grohl over to the dark side, Mercyful Fate's King Diamond, Trouble's Eric Wagner, Celtic Frost's Tom G. Warrior; local heroes, Wino, aka Robert Scott Weinrich, frontman of cult LA heroes Saint Vitus; and global superstars Cronos of Newcastle black metal creators Venom, Lee Dorrian of Cathedral, Snake from Canadian progressive metallers Voivod, Max Cavalera of Brazilian thrashers Sepultura, and, finally, Lemmy from Motörhead—an undeniably impressive constellation of the genre's finest.

Opposite: *Probot* gave Grohl a chance to record with heavy metal legends like Motörhead's Lemmy Kilmister.

The singers often recorded their parts remotely, with minimal direction from Grohl. Upon receiving his track, Cavalera thrilled to its close resemblance to the insurrectionary sounds of his old group's landmark 1993 album *Chaos A.D.* wrote his track in the flavor of that album, making it "more political, about war and chaos." Cronos took so well to his track—the opening, devil-driven dash of "Centuries Of Sin"—that his band Venom added it to their live set, while Cavalera's band Soulfly has also played his furnace-throated punk-metal gallop of "Red War" on tour.

Grohl often tailored the tracks to fit the proposed vocalist, so "Shake Your Blood" was penned in the image of Lemmy's band Motörhead, right down to the "Ace Of Spades" three syllable hook, and "Access Babylon" achieving the brisk tempos that characterized the crossover-thrash era of Mike Dean's Corrosion of Conformity. The album's breadth of styles and textures, meanwhile, spoke to the ambition and creativity of this era of metal, encompassing the proggy majesty of "Ice Cold Man" (featuring Lee Dorrian), and the Bowie-esque swagger of Eric Warner's "My Tortured Soul," and the gloriously out-there dramas of the closing "Sweet Dreams," sung by King Diamond. A hidden twelfth track would break *Probot*'s cardinal rule, featuring a contemporary singer, but Jack Black's note-perfect vamp on the classic metal vocal on "I Am A Warlock" comes from a very sincere but also very funny place.

Left: *Probot* offered Grohl a chance to reconnect with his metal roots and prove he could rock as hard and heavy as any of his contemporaries.

Right: Corrosion of Conformity, who expertly straddled the line between heavy metal and hardcore punk throughout the 1980s.

> "When I had a riff I thought was pretty good, I'd peek over at Jimmy. If he was just watching TV, then it sucked. But if he looked over, then I knew it was a keeper."
>
> **DAVE GROHL**

Embracing its concept without flinching, and watering the source material down not one iota, *Probot* offered precious few points of access for the metal-phobic Foos aficionados; this was one for the metal-heads. Released on Southern Lord, a tiny independent label run by Greg Anderson of Goatsnake and Sunn O))) that specialized in experimental metal and was home to the underground likes of Om, Sleep, and Pelican, *Probot* nevertheless reached the UK Top 40, and number sixty-eight on the US *Billboard* charts. It was warmly received by the metal critics. And, perhaps most importantly, it allowed Grohl to decisively scratch his metal itch, and make his peace with "Learn To Fly."

Reactionary phase complete, he was now free to return to Foo Fighting duty, and begin work on their fifth album. But first he had to build himself a new studio again, as Dave Grohl's life was about to weather another great change.

It's August 2, 2003, and at the $2 million Los Angeles villa he purchased that April, Dave Grohl is overseeing his grandest project yet: his wedding to fiancée Jordyn Blum, an undertaking requiring new carpeting, lights, chandeliers, and a thorough spring-cleaning of the Grohl gaff. Grohl had just returned from a US tour with Foo Fighters, and the group were about to set off to Europe to play the festival circuit, but in this brief window in his schedule, he found time to marry Jordyn, in a tent the size of "the main tent at the Reading festival," located on the villa's tennis court.

Grohl had first met Blum earlier in the decade, at a whiskey bar in Los Angeles. Grohl was reluctantly dragged along to the

Foo Fighters: The Band That Dave Made

Opposite: A second swing at marriage, to Jordyn Blum, would deliver Grohl the happiness and stability he was yearning for, along with a family.

bar, where waitresses wear bunny outfits, by a friend who was dating one of those waitresses. Not really wanting to be there, he arrived in a T-shirt and "disgusting shorts," and Jordyn, the friend of the waitress Grohl's buddy was dating, was hardly impressed by what she saw. Grohl, very much impressed by Jordyn, bought copious drinks for their party to break the ice, but in the end chose to make his feelings towards Blum known by scrawling "You're my future ex-wife" on a piece of paper with his phone number and handing it to her.

They dated, though Grohl was still pursuing a bachelor life, and he called time on the relationship before things got too serious. Hawkins's overdose, however, made Grohl re-examine his life. "It was an epiphany where I realized life is very delicate," Grohl told *NME* in 2003. "It's too short to wait for anything to happen to you. It's too short to waste on anything superficial and unimportant. You have to fill your days with things that are meaningful and real."

When Grohl returned to LA, he called Blum and invited her out for a drink. She arrived grinning, sporting a wedding ring (a joke meant to unnerve Grohl) "and we've been together ever since," Grohl told *Elle* magazine.

That August afternoon, with Jimmy Swanson serving as usher, Krist Novoselic and Tenacious D's Jack Black and Kyle Gass in the room, and Taylor Hawkins at hand, Grohl and Blum wed, and began married life traveling to Europe, and another batch of Foo Fighters shows, though Grohl had his eye on starting a family sooner rather than later. He soon began putting down some serious Los Angeles roots, relocating his beloved Studio 606 from Alexandria to the West Coast. But this new Studio 606 wouldn't be some modest basement with sleeping bags hanging from the walls.

Located ten minutes from Grohl's home, in Northridge, a neighborhood in the San Fernando Valley, the new Studio 606 West was eight-thousand feet of wood-paneled studio luxury hiding behind an unassuming suburban facade.

Beyond the wood paneling, it heaves with Grohl-related Gold and Platinum discs, and iconic photography of iconic musicians, and old Black Flag poster-bills, and a noisy Addams Family pinball machine (though Grohl is strictly all about the ping-pong when he's at the studio) like some dream man-cave. But the studio has a lot going on under the hood, stocked with vintage, rare-as-hen's-teeth, and blisteringly expensive recording gear, which would later include the very Neve desk Nirvana recorded *Nevermind* on, purchased by Grohl after the old Sound City studio closed in 2011.

It's here that Dave Grohl will write and record the fifth Foo Fighters album, *In Your Honor,* a sprawling, epic, sonically diverse set that will end up spanning two compact discs, and see Grohl collaborating with artists from far outside his usual sphere of reference.

When Grohl started work on *In Your Honor*, his intention was not to start work on a fifth Foo Fighters album. He'd only just completed touring *One by One*, and his confidence in the band was riding high. "We'd finally established ourselves to the point where we could play an hour and a half set and make 50,000 people sing all the words," he told the *Independent*. But it had been a grueling slog towards the end. "I'm thirty-six now, and I've been doing it for eighteen years. Is this what I'm supposed to do with the rest of my life? I don't know. Maybe it's time to have the band take another turn."

So *In Your Honor* began not as an album, but as something, anything else. First it was sketched out as a film soundtrack, in the vein of old bandmate Tom Petty's work for the 1996 romcom

> "It was an epiphany where I realized life is very delicate. It's too short to wait for anything to happen to you. It's too short to waste on anything superficial and unimportant. You have to fill your days with things that are meaningful and real."
>
> **DAVE GROHL**

She's the One; working in the acoustic medium on these songs, Grohl decided the group should make an unplugged album of new material. And then Grohl quickly realized he would miss playing electric guitar on the album. So now the plan was to pile into the studio and record everything they had, as wide a sprawl of music as they could compose, and get as much of it onto the album. Make it two albums, if necessary. Let's make it special.

This creative overdrive was powered, in part, by Grohl's abiding opinion of *One by One*. The album had received some strong reviews in the media, but there were other voices suggesting it was a disappointment. The online pop culture site *A.V. Club* classed much of the album as "middling, sticking to slick, pounding, functional rock that doesn't dig much deeper than the usual spleen-venting and loud-quiet brooding-to-bluster formula." The album had scooped the 2004 Grammy for Best Rock Album, a year after "All My Life" won Best Hard Rock Performance, topped the UK charts, and reached number three on *Billboard* in the US, selling a million copies in the US alone—a figure not to be sniffed at, as internet file sharing began to bite rock's bottom end.

Still, Grohl was unsatisfied with the album, haunted by the way they had raced to put it together, following the earlier, failed sessions. "I regret that," he said later, "cos I knew that we were capable of doing better." The new Foos album, then, would be an orgy of over-achievement, an exercise in trying harder. "It's inevitable that, in every band's career, they get the itch to do the pretentious, 'White Album'-style freak-out," he told interviewers, in the run-up to the new album's release, referencing The Beatles' own 1968 untitled album, a sprawling, diverse, occasionally mystifying, and always mercurial double set.

Grohl had been promising the Foos' own 'White Album' folly since *The Colour and the Shape*, and that was the standard the Foos' fifth would strive for. Ambitious stuff. But, as Grohl had discovered, you get nowhere aiming for anything but the best.

"We came into the studio with five and a half hours of music," Grohl remembered later. "The idea wasn't to get experimental, it was to make two great records that would stand on their own." By the time sessions began in the newly completed Studio 606

Left: Foo Fighters performing at the 46th Annual Grammy Awards in 2004, after collecting the second Best Rock Album Grammy of their career, for *One by One*.

Opposite: *In Your Honor* would offer Taylor Hawkins an opportunity to swap the drums for a microphone, singing "Cold Day In The Sun."

Below: Norah Jones guested on *In Your Honor*'s acoustic disc, duetting with Grohl on the haunting "Virginia Moon."

West, the concept for the new album had evolved to a double album, with one disc electric, and the other acoustic. Grohl anticipated apprehension from the group's paymasters, who might expect the group could use the double album length to deliver "Eighty-five minutes of pretentious bullshit." But that wasn't how Grohl rolled, and the album would contain some of Grohl's most painstakingly crafted music.

"When we started recording the acoustic half of the album, we had no idea what was going to happen; we'd never done anything like that before," Grohl told me, shortly before *In Your Honor*'s release, in spring, 2005. He might not have been aiming to make an explicitly experimental record, but in stripping away the amplification and distortion and dynamics that were key elements of so much Foos music, disc two of *In Your Honor* was a step into the unknown for the group. The nineties was, of course, the era of *MTV Unplugged*, the hit show where various venerated electric musicians performed acoustic versions of

their work, and spin-off albums from the show went on to be smash hits for the likes of Eric Clapton, Neil Young, and, yes, Nirvana (though Cobain initially did not invite Grohl to perform at their *Unplugged* session, relenting later).

But Foo Fighters' acoustic record was a grander project than just taping old man Grohl and his guitar. "When we first started playing the acoustic record, most people were under the impression that it would just be my vocal and an acoustic guitar throughout," Grohl said. "But while all of these songs began with an acoustic guitar and a vocal, from there we just started building. If it needed another guitar, we'd throw another one on. If it needed a slide guitar, or accordions, or pump organs, or mellotrons, or violins. . .We would just take each song to the point where we felt that they were done. We could have gone even farther than we did, but the fact that we had imagined an acoustic record kept us from going too far, most of the time."

The acoustic half would contain one of Grohl's most tender, sweet-hearted songs to date, "Virginia Moon," a swoonsome strum with more than a little Ipanema swing in its bones, a deliriously beautiful duet with then-reigning queen of easy listening Norah Jones. "On The Mend"—originally penned in a London hotel room—was a lulling, meditative number, with some unexpected and wonderful chord changes. "What If I Do" was another ruminative thing, a kindred spirit to *There's Nothing Left to Lose*'s "M.I.A." in subject. The eddying shanty "Another Round" welcomed another celebrity guest to the sessions—Led Zeppelin bassist John Paul Jones, who'd since pursued a career as a producer and arranger, and played mandolin on the track, and added piano to the ravishing "Miracle." "I just sat in the control room, remembering the times I'd dropped acid listening to [Led Zeppelin track] 'Going To California,'" recalled a star-struck Grohl.

The acoustic half of *In Your Honor* contained some of the album's lightest moments, not least "Cold Day In The Sun," penned and sung by Taylor Hawkins, who blesses its wry Byrdsian jangle with his Tom Petty croak. But it would be foolish to imagine that because it used no electricity, it had no bite. Opener "Still" was, Grohl explained, "The first song I wrote that came close to any sort of story-telling." It was inspired by a memory from Grohl's youth, of hearing swarms of siren-ringing ambulances tearing about his neighborhood; later, Grohl would discover that a local teen had lain down on the railroad tracks and committed suicide. That unease and foreboding plays out in the reverb-soaked ambiance, the edgy burr of the organ, that ever-tightening guitar figure, and Grohl's own whispered vocals, unfurling the narrative, and a sense of doomed resignation. "After the ambulances split, we found pieces of skull and we played with his bones," Grohl told *Rolling Stone*, of the incident that inspired the track. "The acoustic album runs deep."

That it does—heavy, though never metal, and leavened with enough melodic grace as to always remain eminently listenable.

Opposite: Bassist Nate Mendel, October 4, 2005, University of Illinois, USA

Closing track "Razor," penned while Grohl was performing at a benefit for the 2004 tsunami relief efforts, complements its darkly mysterious lyric with a tense guitar accompaniment (the rhythm part is played by a guesting Josh Homme). But the most haunting and intense track on *In Your Honor* was a song Grohl had written a decade-and-a-half earlier, and recorded for the *Pocketwatch* album. "Friend Of A Friend" was penned while staying in Kurt Cobain's Olympia apartment, shortly after he'd taken on the role of drummer with Nirvana, and it reads like a diary entry, Grohl reflecting on the new friends he's making, with no sense of how important an influence they'll be on his life, or where fate will take them.

"That song is so old," Grohl told me in 2005. "I'd written songs before, for Scream, and in my friend's basement for fun. But when I wrote 'Friend Of A Friend,' that was the first time I'd written something so naked. And I was into it. I've listened to music like Ry Cooder's soundtrack to *Paris, Texas*, and the third Led Zeppelin album, all my life—that music soundtracked my dropping out of high school and hitting the road. I love the fragile side of music as much as the bombastic loudness. I wrote that song just after moving to Olympia, when I moved in with Kurt. There were nights there when it was so quiet; Kurt was in his bedroom writing lyrics or journals or poetry or whatever, and I was on the couch." It was this haunted, unexpectedly deft side of Foo Fighters displayed on *In Your Honor* that made it such a striking album. Grohl understood that the "rock" album had to do more than simply crank the amplifiers up to eleven in order to catch the attention of listeners. "The way we made the 'rock' record was a lot like we made the last record," Nate said, but the songs of *In Your Honor* displayed a renewed focus, a higher standard of inspiration than its predecessor. When it riffed hard—which was often—it pushed beyond the comfort zone, playing to the extremes, repeating until they drew blood. The scale of this new music was key—"With the rock album, there were, like, eighty tracks on everything," Grohl said, noting the importance of overdubs to build the colossal walls of electric guitar that scored the album. Opening track "In Your Honor" stirred those endless layers of guitars in service of a sound that was epic, fierce, and yet strangely gentle: hitting some perfect zone of volume and grandiose tranquility, like Sonic Youth or Mogwai. The song—which grew and grew, until slipping into a wild double-time vamos at the end—was an unabashed anthem,

Best Of You

> "I'd written songs before, for Scream, and in my friend's basement for fun. But when I wrote 'Friend Of A Friend,' that was the first time I'd written something so naked. I love the fragile side of music as much as the bombastic loudness."
>
> **DAVE GROHL**

which Taylor said was dedicated "to our fans, our audience, really—we're gonna rip our hearts out for you," like Jagger's onstage suicide in the old Stones' hit "It's Only Rock 'n Roll." Elsewhere, "Free Me" put those guitars to work on a punk-metal cyclone, with Grohl's gladiatorial howl the only thing anchoring it to the ground, while "Resolve" sweetened the din with some melodic heroism. "End Over End," meanwhile, closed the album with an elliptical hard-rock piledriver built around an unforgettable hook.

But the finest of the "rock" album's entries was "Best Of You." Penned early in the sessions, the song had gotten discarded somewhere along *In Your Honor*'s extended production. But as the album came to completion, manager John Silva questioned Grohl as to what had happened to "that 'Best Of You' song?" A masterpiece of soaring, emotive melody and sensitive volume, it was as unabashedly anthemic as anything Foo Fighters had yet recorded.

"Most people think it's a love song, but it's more universal," Grohl later recalled. The roots of the song lay in rallies Grohl performed at in support of John Kerry, the Democratic presidential candidate and George W. Bush's challenger in the 2004 US elections. "I would play acoustic shows at these rallies, and nobody knew who I was," Grohl remembered, to the *Independent*'s Craig McLean. "What inspired me most wasn't necessarily political. It was the strength of community and human will. Seeing so many people come out because they either desperately needed to be rescued or they genuinely wanted change. It really hit me. I'd never been so deeply involved in something so important. It was unbelievably inspirational."

The song asked listeners, "Were you born to resist, or be abused?" Politics had never played an explicit part in Foo

Opposite: Dave Grohl of Foo Fighters onstage at Rod Laver Arena, Melbourne, Australia, December 7, 2005

Right: Led Zeppelin's brilliant, often-acoustic third album helped give Grohl the confidence to embrace his softer side on *In Your Honor*.

 "What inspired me most wasn't necessarily political. It was the strength of community and human will. It was unbelievably inspirational."
DAVE GROHL

John Kerry's (center) presidential campaign saw Grohl make explicit his political leanings, and inspired the new album's "Best Of You."

Above: Foo Fighters, Australia, 2005. (L-R) Nate Mendel, Dave Grohl, Chris Shiflett, Taylor Hawkins

Fighters' art before, but desperate times called for strong measures, and Grohl's Foos were ever a band in transition, as *In Your Honor* proved. "This album has made it so there are no boundaries for this band, at all," Grohl said, his pride in this remarkable work showing through.

Ten years on from Foo Fighters' birth, Grohl is well-positioned to look back and take stock of his stardom, and consider how his old friend Kurt had struggled with the same: "I never didn't want it," he told me, "I just never expected it. Nirvana never had that

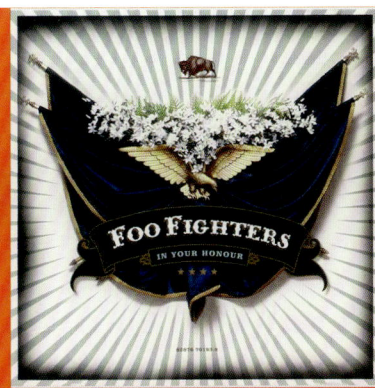

In Your Honor

Released: June 14, 2005
Label: Roswell/RCA
Recorded: January–March, 2005
Studio 606 West, Northridge, Los Angeles

PERSONNEL:
Dave Grohl: lead vocals, backing vocals, rhythm guitar, percussion, drums on "Cold Day In The Sun"
Nate Mendel: bass
Taylor Hawkins: drums, percussion, lead vocals and rhythm guitar on "Cold Day In The Sun"
Chris Shiflett: lead guitar

Additional personnel:
Joe Beebe: guitar on "Virginia Moon"
Danny Clinch: harmonica on "Another Round"
Petra Haden: violin on "Miracle"
Josh Homme: rhythm guitar on "Razor"
John Paul Jones: mandolin on "Another Round" and piano on "Miracle"
Rami Jaffee: keyboards on "Still," "What If I Do?," "Another Round," "Over And Out," "On The Mend" and "Cold Day In The Sun"
Norah Jones: vocals and piano on "Virginia Moon"
Nick Raskulinecz: production, double bass on "On The Mend" and bass on "Cold Day In The Sun"

TRACK LISTING:
All tracks written by Dave Grohl, Taylor Hawkins, Nate Mendel, and Chris Shiflett except where noted

DISC ONE
1. "In Your Honor"
2. "No Way Back"
3. "Best Of You"
4. "DOA"
5. "Hell"
6. "The Last Song"
7. "Free Me"
8. "Resolve"
9. "The Deepest Blues Are Black"
10. "End Over End"

DISC TWO
1. "Still"
2. "What If I Do?"
3. "Miracle"
4. "Another Round"
5. "Friend Of A Friend" (Grohl)
6. "Over And Out"
7. "On The Mend"
8. "Virginia Moon"
9. "Cold Day In The Sun" (Hawkins)
10. "Razor" (Grohl)

'world domination' career ambition, because our kind of music made it impossible that we could be the biggest band in the world. When I joined Nirvana, it was for the same reason I joined Scream: for the music. That's where people get fucked up, when they have that insane ambition and expectation. If music's not enough on its own, don't do it. There's no way I'd let a guitar sit around and gather dust, there's no way. The most embarrassing question I could be asked is, what do you do other than music? Because I don't have any interests outside music.

"Every record we've made I always imagined being the last," Grohl concluded. "I've thought, what a fucking amazing run. I feel like the luckiest guy in the world, that I get to do all this amazing shit. Whether it's jamming with some of the coolest bands in the world, or building a beautiful studio or recording a double album, I can't imagine being any more blessed than I already am. For once in my life I've made a record I don't want to be the last. It's opening doors I can see through for ten more years. And that's never happened before."

Foo Fighters, Sydney, 2006. (L-R) Taylor Hawkins, Dave Grohl, Nate Mendel, Chris Shiflett

Stranger Things Have Happened

"The key to longevity is balance. I love this band like a family. But I've realized that the most important thing is my life outside the band. Without this, everything else would fall apart."

DAVE GROHL

As one might expect for such an elaborate, ambitious album, touring *In Your Honor* would prove an elaborate, ambitious undertaking. The first leg was relatively traditional, as the Foos spent their summer the way they often did, trekking across Europe, tracing the festival circuit. The difference this time was they'd now ascended to the dizzying heights of headliners, including 2005's Reading Festival, closing the main stage on the Saturday night a decade after their riotous performance in the big tent. Following the European festivals, the Foos co-headlined a jaunt across America with nervy power-pop quartet Weezer—billed, jokingly, as the "Foozer" tour—where they played their hits and the cream of the electric material from *In Your Honor*, before returning to Europe on their own, for a tour that took them through to the early weeks of 2006.

The group took that spring off from rocking, though these would prove busy months for Grohl, who became a father for the first time on April 15, when Jordyn gave birth to their daughter, Violet Maye. Perhaps reflecting the needs of a man newly acquainted with the realities of sleepless nights scored by a screaming newborn, when the Foos returned to duty that summer, the group presented a markedly gentler in-concert proposition than before. Sure, a brief blitz across the UK that June witnessed the traditional Foo Fighters heavy rock show, in the form of two mega-huge concerts at London's Hyde Park and Manchester's Old Trafford cricket ground; the former was their biggest show to date, graced by all-star special guests like

Right: The band's concert in London's Hyde Park in June 2006 was the biggest show they'd played so far in their career.

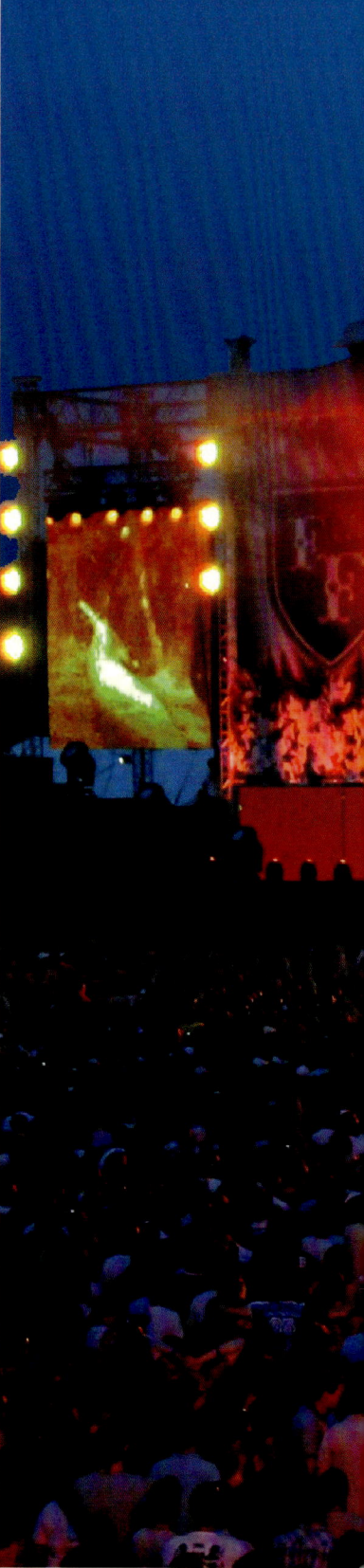

Below: Foo Fighters returned to the Reading Festival in 2005—this time as headliners on the main stage.

> "It didn't feel like the most important show of our career. It was more like I was hosting a barbecue for 85,000 people."
> **DAVE GROHL**

Foo Fighters: The Band That Dave Made

"I was wary of Pat. I think anybody would have been. He almost came back after I'd been in the band a month. And I would have been out at that point, it wasn't like now. I didn't have my footing. So that was my frame of mind: here's this guy who wants my job and my job is how I feed my children and pay my rent."

CHRIS SHIFLETT

Lemmy, stepping up for a ferocious tear through his *Probot* banger "Shake Your Blood," and Queen's Roger Taylor and Brian May for an encore of "We Will Rock You" and "Tie Your Mother Down." A big night for the band, though Grohl didn't let any sense of ceremony intrude upon his having a good time, grilling chicken and steak for his friends in the backstage area, before walking onstage. "It didn't feel like the most important show of our career," Grohl said later. "It was more like I was hosting a barbecue for 85,000 people."

But, several days before those shows, and following their performance at the Isle of Wight Festival, the Foos moseyed up to the Regent Theatre in Ipswich, eighty miles north-east of London, to play a secret show displaying a striking change of gear. That night, Grohl, Hawkins, Mendel, and Shiflett toted acoustic guitars, or brushes where they might previously have used drumsticks, and brought with them several extra musicians to bolster this new unplugged presentation. On violin was Petra Haden, daughter of esteemed jazz bassist and bandleader Charlie, and formerly a member of underrated indie-rock group That Dog; on keyboards, Rami Jaffee, of Jakob Dylan's band The Wallflowers; on percussion, sessioneer Drew Hester; and on extra guitar, none other than former Nirvana and Foo Fighters sideman Pat Smear, making his return to the fold.

The Ipswich show was a dry run for a performance two nights later at the Apollo Victoria Theatre in London, debuting the acoustic show the group would soon tour across America. Grohl walked onto the Apollo stage alone that night, dressed all in black, and began playing "Razor" on his own, with the augmented Foos joining him for the final verse. Their set that night drew mostly from *In Your Honor*, with Haden delivering Norah Jones's vocal on the bossa nova "Virginia Moon," and Hawkins getting to sing his "Cold Day In The Sun," though some Foos classics also surfaced, albeit in stripped-back form. There were luminous takes of "Walking Away From You" and "Next Year," and a haunting "Ain't It The Life," while Haden sang co-vocals on "Floaty." At one point, Grohl threatened to play "All My Life," the face-stomping opener from the *One By One* album, before catching himself; "I'm only joking," he grinned, "there's no way we're doing an acoustic version of that shit." The encore, meanwhile, saw Grohl alone, strumming "Friend Of A Friend" and "Best Of You," before the band rejoined him for a closing "Everlong."

A triumph, the Apollo show set the template for the acoustic shows the Foo Fighters would perform across America for the rest of the summer, where the set list expanded to include Grohl's sole songwriting contribution to Nirvana, "Marigold," and a searing take on "My Hero." On the version captured on their 2006 live album, *Skin and Bones*, culled from the group's three shows at Los Angeles's Pantages Theatre, the wall of three acoustic guitars—played by Grohl, Shiflett, and Smear—compose a sound as heavy and defiant as anything in the Foo Fighters' catalog.

Left: KROQ's 2006 Almost Acoustic Christmas gave the Foo Fighters a chance to air their unplugged material—though Shiflett warily eyed a returning Smear.

Left: Incoming keyboard player Rami Jaffee (far left) alongside his former bandmates in Jakob Dylan and The Wallflowers

The trio's guitars sounded great together on this tour, but the truth was that Smear's return to the Foos' touring ranks wasn't without teething pains. Shiflett, for one, later admitted feeling anxious and a little displaced as a result of his predecessor rejoining the group, explaining that, from the earliest days of his tenure with the Foos, he was aware that Smear was occasionally in conversations with Grohl about returning. "I was wary of Pat," Shiflett said. "I think anybody would have been. He almost came back after I'd been in the band a month. And I would have been out at that point, it wasn't like now. I didn't have my footing. So that was my frame of mind: here's this guy who wants my job and my job is how I feed my children and pay my rent. So my job's important to me for lots of reasons, musically and otherwise."

Shiflett quickly realized that he had nothing to fear from Smear's return, however, and, as the two guitarists soon became firm friends, it seemed that the choppy waters that had plagued the Foo Fighters line-up in its earliest days had finally calmed.

The acoustic tour was a triumph, Grohl stepping firmly outside of his anthemic-rock comfort zone and locating a new vocabulary for his music. But the Foos didn't spend much of 2006 on the road, playing only fifty-five shows that year, while the following year would see only forty-four performances. The truth was that now he had become a father, Grohl had no desire to miss out on Violet's childhood by pursuing his life as a touring rock hellion. "No more than two weeks out on the road, that's the new rule," he told old friend Keith Cameron in the *Guardian*. "No more six-month tours."

Of course, Grohl admitted, he was blessed to be in a position where he was financially stable and could choose whether or not, and when, he went on tour. Similarly, when it came time to start writing and recording what would become Foo Fighters' sixth studio album, Grohl was lucky enough to have a place of his own, Studio 606 West, where he could rough out demos and work on the new material at his own pace and to his own timetable—and his record of consistent commercial success meant he didn't have to worry about the record label intruding upon his creativity and offering unwanted "advice" on the direction the group should take. "We've built this little world," Grohl told *Clash* magazine, "with our own studio and our own label, and directing our own videos and finding our own producers. We're able to walk into our fortress, Studio 606, and lock the door and turn everything outside off, and I think that's helped us survive."

Still, this didn't mean that Grohl wasn't open to the occasional gem of wisdom from his corporate paymasters— especially when those paymasters came in the form of RCA's then-president Clive Davis, an internationally renowned record mogul who had played a crucial role in the careers of artists as diverse as Bruce Springsteen, Aerosmith, Whitney Houston, and Barry Manilow. One evening when their paths crossed, Grohl found himself reflecting upon the recent Foo Fighters tours, the purely acoustic tour and the mostly electric tour that preceded it, and how those shows appealed to different audiences. And Davis said, simply, that the group could play both their acoustic and electric songs and draw those different audiences together; they didn't have to choose between the two. It was a simple concept, but revelatory enough for Grohl that it would define his approach for this sixth album, which was to take those two diverse sides of the Foo Fighters muse given space on *In Your Honor*, and fuse them together somehow; to produce music as powerful and tender and muscular and complex as that sprawling double album, but with a newfound concision.

Certainly, after the success of *In Your Honor* and the acoustic tour, Grohl felt a certain invincible swagger, possessed of enough confidence to attempt something that hadn't played out so well the last time he tried it. Once the group were ready to begin recording the new album, Grohl grabbed his Rolodex and once again got in contact with Gil Norton, producer of the tough, tension-filled *The Colour and the Shape* sessions. Recording began in March 2007 at Studio 606, with Norton in the control room; thankfully, however, it was quickly clear that the vexatious vibes that had plagued the recording of *The Colour and the Shape* had dissipated.

"It was really good to work with him again," Nate Mendel said later. "Gil's great at what he does. Gil's a bass-player, and he was really into trying to come up with interesting bass lines. He was like a coach in that direction."

The feeling was mutual for Norton. "Nate is one of the best bass players in the world," he said. "He works so hard—during the sessions, he would go away and sit with his bass, constantly playing to a backing track. He's a great musician." His first working experience with Hawkins impressed Norton, too, and made it clear Norton would not experience the same difficulties he had had with William Goldsmith. "He's a great drummer, and he's confident in his own abilities," he said, of Hawkins. "He's still not 'Grohl-good'—but he knows he is the Foo Fighters' drummer, end of conversation."

Right: The arrival of Grohl's first child, Violet, signaled changes in the way he lived— and in how the Foo Fighters would operate in the future.

> "It was really good to work with him again. Gil's great at what he does. Gil's a bass-player, and he was really into trying to come up with interesting bass lines. He was like a coach in that direction."
>
> **NATE MENDEL**

Grohl's ambition, entering the studio, was to create an album that wasn't as schizophrenic as *In Your Honor*—to make a record which, above all, made sense as an album. It was here that Norton's input was crucial; whereas Nick Raskulinecz, who'd produced *One By One* and *In Your Honor*, was happy to sit back and let Grohl direct proceedings, the more proactive Norton challenged Grohl's decisions, questioned his song choices, and second-guessed his instincts, resulting in an altogether more lively and creative production experience. "Gil is the one rock producer that we're compatible with, because he's unconventional," Grohl told *Kerrang!*. "He seems to capture the best of this band."

"The last couple of records have really been co-produced by Dave," Mendel added. "He's been there the whole time, making all the final decisions. Gil's been a little bit more 'in charge,' and Dave's been able to pull back a little, and not have to make all the decisions and oversee everything."

Norton arrived at Studio 606 and spent the first week sorting through demos of thirty to forty freshly penned Foos anthems. "We just picked the most powerful, dramatic songs," remembered Grohl. "If we had a beautiful melody, we'd throw a fucking string quartet in there. We did everything we could to really magnify all those elements, and that was fun. There was no fear of going too far."

Grohl embraced the challenge of striking a balance between Foo Fighters' punk rock instincts and their more mature, gentle side. He spoke of songs that went from "four-piece rock band shit" to middle sections that turn "into this mass orchestrated swarm and ridiculous time signatures," and how it had "always been my dream to mix Steely Dan with Nomeansno." Certainly, this was the first time the Dan—the slick seventies rock band who swung like jazzbos and whose harmony-laden pop boasted the finest musicianship in the industry—had been even mentioned in the same breath as anarchic Canadian avant-punks Nomeansno. And if the resulting album—titled *Echoes, Silence, Patience & Grace*, after a lyric from closing song "Home," which Grohl declared "the best song I've ever written"—perhaps struggled to evoke such a violent soundclash, it represented their best distillation yet of the band's (or, more specifically, Grohl's) divergent influences.

Norton's production rarely relied on simple loudness to indicate heaviness, preferring a more nuanced, sophisticated sense of dynamics. But when the album rocked, it rocked hard. "Erase/Replace's" blast beats and furious fusillades of guitars were an unabashed callback to thrash metal titans Metallica, and the hours a teenaged Grohl spent rocking out with Jimmy Swanson. "I still listen to *Kill 'Em All* once a week, and there's a part of me that will never lose the love for riffs," Grohl told *Kerrang!*, adding that his parallel career as a drummer was a

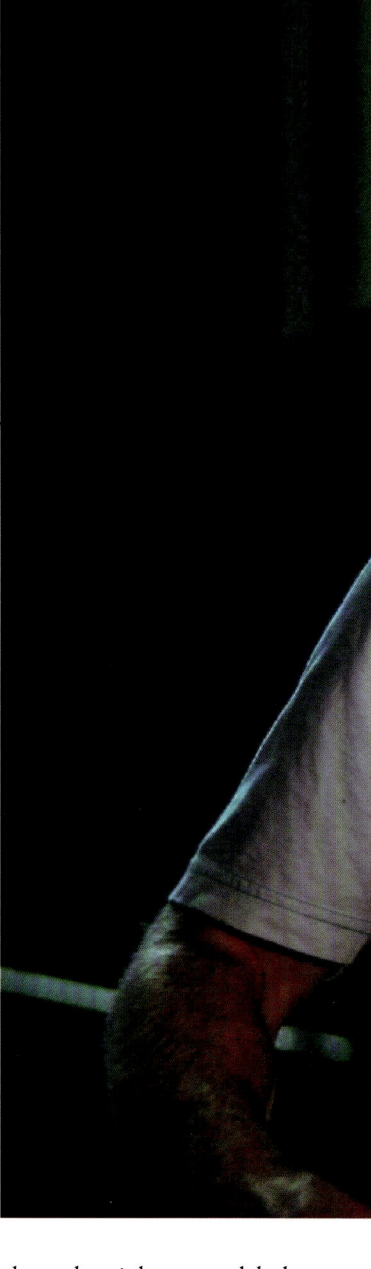

Right: Nate Mendel performs onstage on June 10, 2006, at the Nokia Isle of Wight Festival, Seaclose Park, Newport, England.

boon for his riff-writing endeavors. "As a drummer and a guitar player, the rhythmic quality of a decent riff means I can write riffs all day long, because I look at the guitar like a drum set. Just as I'll sit at a drum set and play beats, I sit with a guitar and try the same thing."

The riff of "Erase/Replace," then, saw Grohl hammer at his guitar with the fury of a million Dave Lombardos, though its blitzing was elevated by an eerie, nagging guitar hook out of late-period Pixies, and a brooding, post-rock-meets-soft-rock middle section. But while slow burner "Let It Die" reached ear-melting levels of intensity, tonally the rest of the album was everything Grohl promised: varied, textured, complex.

"Statues" might not have boasted sardonic Pynchon-esque lyrics or guitar from Jeff "Skunk" Baxter, but its easy-going glide was as close as Foo Fighters were ever going to satisfy their Steely Dan fetish. The likes of "Long Road To Ruin" and "Summer's End," meanwhile, proved Grohl a master of a particular form of rock songwriting, where the muscle was matched by melodic sophistication—an update of the seventies rock paradigm, fed through the prism of the rock era in which Grohl came of age, but never imprisoned within grunge's sonic limitations. It was a game Grohl had been playing since *There Is Nothing Left to Lose*: abandoning the sense of the pre-punk and post-punk eras as an insoluble binary, and instead letting the side of him that grew

who doesn't want to leave his family to go touring the world for months. "Every direction leads me away," Grohl murmurs, over muted piano. "All I want, is to be home."

"The key to longevity is balance," Grohl told *Spin* magazine, as the album hit shelves. "I love this band like a family. But I've realized that the most important thing is my life outside the band. Without this, everything else would fall apart." Fatherhood had let him know that his own time on the planet was finite, and the clock was ticking. But rather than let this knowledge paralyze him with fear, Grohl used it to push himself forward, and risk new things with his art. "After a while, you lose your insecurities," he said, "and you think, 'Man, I only up loving seventies AM radio live peacefully alongside the part of him that moshed at hardcore shows. These poles didn't need to be in conflict; Foo Fighters' sixth album was an ambitious beast that made perfect bedfellows of them.

Left: The plight of Tasmanian miners Todd Russell (left) and Brant Webb (right), trapped underground for two weeks, inspired "Ballad Of The Beaconsfield Miners."

Right: Guitarist and composer Kaki King lent her considerable talents to the studio recording of "Ballad Of The Beaconsfield Miners."

The album got downright folky in its final quarter. "Ballad Of The Beaconsfield Miners" was dedicated to Brant Webb and Todd Russell, two workers who found themselves trapped in a Tasmanian gold mine following an earthquake. Stuck underground for a fortnight, facing likely death, the pair requested an iPod filled with the Foos' music to be sent down, to pass their time in their underground purgatory. Word reached Grohl, who, affected by their plight, sent them a fax, reading, "Though I'm halfway round the world right now, my heart is with you both, and I want you to know that when I come home, there's two tickets to any Foos show, anywhere, and two cold beers waiting for you. Deal?" After they were rescued, one of the miners took Grohl up on his offer, sharing a beer with Grohl after the Foos' set at the Sydney Opera House in October, 2006. In their honor, Grohl composed the instrumental piece, accompanied by guests, virtuoso pedal steel guitarist Kaki King, and a visiting Pat Smear. Grohl said he was moved to record the piece because the miners' request for Foos music "made me feel for maybe the first time that what we do is good, and that it can help people."

This last quarter of the album found Grohl introspective, downbeat, meditative. He was thirty-eight and, like every other member of Foo Fighters, a father. Life had taken on a new meaning, been filled with a new kind of joy—but his sense of mortality was perhaps keener and more bittersweet now. "To dust, as everything must, we fade away," he mused, on "Statues." "Home," meanwhile was very much the rumination of a dad

have a short time here, and I wanna do as much as I can.'"

He was perhaps more in touch with his muse than he'd ever been, and yet in this moment he could also see a time when he wouldn't be a Foo Fighter, or even a rock star. "I don't imagine it will last forever," he reflected to *Clash* magazine. "There are times when I could imagine just being a stay-at-home dad, you know? The days I don't go to the studio it's a good fuckin' sixteen-hour day of just being a father, and—it's great man. You get her down at night, you sit down on the couch and you think of all the shit that you did that day. It's a great feeling; you're exhausted, but. . .To me it seems like the idea is to stretch your days. Who knows how long you're gonna live, so why not try to get as much in as you can? A full day with a sixteen-month-old baby is a fuckin' full day! When you go to sleep you go down hard!"

There would be no more epic multi-month trips across the globe for Foo Fighters, at least not while their kids were still young. So, when Foo Fighters played shows now, they would be on a grand scale. They would go big, and then they would go home.

A couple of months before *Echoes, Silence, Patience & Grace*'s September 2007 release date, the Foos performed at *Live Earth*, a series of benefit concerts taking place at eleven locations across the globe on July 7, in aid of climate protection charities, and

"Roger said Wembley was fuckin' huge. And when someone from Queen says the place is fuckin' huge, that means it's fuckin' huge. It comes down to breaking that barrier from the stage to the audience, and making everyone feel involved. When we play live, it's important that we're all connected in that way."

DAVE GROHL

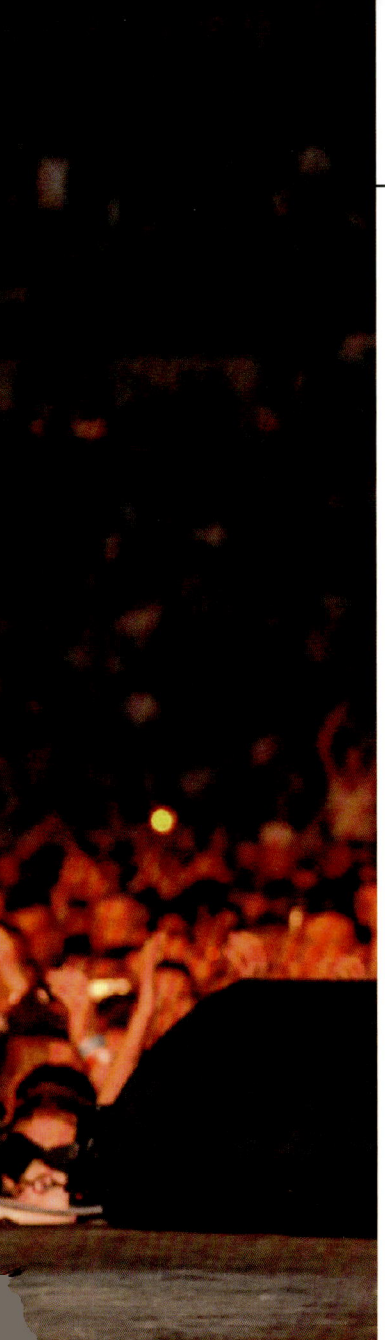

Left: Foo Fighters' appearance at the 2007 *Live Earth* concert gave Grohl a taste for the vastness of Wembley Stadium.

to raise awareness of global warning. Joining Metallica, Beastie Boys, Red Hot Chili Peppers, and Madonna at London's Wembley Stadium, the Foo Fighters' performance would be witnessed by millions across the world, including nineteen million viewers in the US alone. It was enough to give even a seasoned road warrior like Grohl a wobble in their confidence.

A couple of days before *Live Earth*, the Foos had played a secret warm-up show at London's Dingwalls (capacity: 500), and, after the show, Grohl pumped his celebrity friend Roger Taylor for advice on how to rock Wembley Stadium (capacity: circa 100,000) as hard as Queen had during their legendary set at Live Aid, twenty-one years earlier. "Roger said Wembley was fuckin' huge," Grohl laughed. "And when someone from Queen says the place is fuckin' huge, that means it's fuckin' huge. I realized that Queen, being one of the greatest live bands of all time, had the ability to shrink somewhere like Wembley Stadium down to the size of Dingwalls, and it was just because Freddie had everyone in the palm of his hand. And it comes down to breaking that barrier from the stage to the audience, and making everyone feel involved. When we play live, it's important that we're all connected in that way."

That July evening, Grohl stepped onstage at Wembley Stadium and did well not to be instantly overawed by the phalanxes of stage lights and video screens, and the sea of people in the audience. As Grohl chugged away at the opening grind of "All My Life," dressed in black and hair down to his shoulders, the TV cameras caught Taylor sneaking a nervous pre-gig smoke at his drum kit. It was their moment to fuck up, but the Foos made it work, Grohl closing out that first verse with an almighty "Wooooaarrrrrghyeaaaaaaaaaahhhh!" kicking his leg high into the air as the song exploded into its rifferific blitzkrieg, turning the thousands of punters in the Wembley Stadium audience into instant moshers. Like Queen all those years before, the Foos triumphed by packing their twenty-five-minute set with all the thrills they usually delivered over two hours, playing the hits perhaps better than they'd ever played them before. Grohl clearly relished taking "All My Life" back down to its ticking-timebomb breakdowns, ratcheting up the tension, like a rollercoaster slowing before that final breakneck dash. "OOOWOOOAAARGH I WANNA SEE EVERYBODY DANCE!" he yelled, like the drill sergeant from Stanley Kubrick's *Full Metal Jacket*. "LET'S GET FUCKIN' WILLLLLLLLLLD!" he added, quick-witted censors blanking out the swear on the live TV feed.

And so the Foos played on, into "My Hero," seemingly propelled solely by their own moxie, and the belief that every time they busted out that massive chorus and Grohl bellowed "C'MON SING ALONG!" that crowd a hundred-thousand strong wouldn't leave him hanging. Grohl even barked at the band to stop playing so the Wembley massive—and they were massive—could take the song on their own. Then the Foos wound the song into some wild freeform thrashalong, Grohl dashing the length of the stage and back, riffing wildly at the same time.

It was, in this moment, impossible not to think of Kurt Cobain, shrinking punk rock violet so painfully uncomfortable in his role as rock frontman, who could never have dreamed of addressing the audience as openly and easily as Grohl did that night, certainly not without some redeeming morsel of cynicism or irony. Grohl hadn't been unwittingly thrust into super-stardom like his tragic friend; as he said, he never didn't want it, and when the time came, Grohl was ready. And there Dave was, owning the moment, risking looking dumb or gauche, revving it up for a good cause. There might have been moments where you wanted to wince for Grohl, like when he dedicated "Times Like These" to organizer and climate campaigner Al

Left: Another album, another Grammy, as the group picked up the Best Rock Album gong for *Echoes, Silence, Patience & Grace*.

Below: Performing at the 2007 MTV Europe Music Awards. The Foo Fighters didn't just play, they hosted the backstage area, interviewing fellow stars too.

Gore by reading the chorus out, deadpan—a bit "on the nose," perhaps. But they were forgettable flashes in a performance that grabbed viewers by the lapel and won them over to the Foos' cause, simply by the strength of Grohl's charisma, the band's gift for fearsome riffage and skyscraper-tall tuneage, and an affecting "Everlong" that made Wembley Stadium feel, well, yes, as intimate as Dingwalls. For the first couple of verses and choruses, Grohl sang and strummed the song unaccompanied at the lip of a gangway that led him to the heart of the Wembley audience, before pausing, soaking up the enormity of the place. Leading the band to rock hard through a final chorus, he leapt up on Hawkins's drum riser in the final seconds and shot a meaningful look to his confrere, the Foo most likely to be digging this high point of classic rock.

The *Live Earth* success sent the Foos off on their pared-back promotional itinerary for *Echoes, Silence, Patience & Grace* with a well-earned swagger, having made one of the world's most legendary stages their own, and in under twenty-five minutes. The achievement helped them convincingly claim ownership of stages across the globe as the months passed, including various festivals across the UK, the MTV Music Video Awards in Vegas, the studio for TV's *Saturday Night Live,* and, into 2008, the fiftieth Grammy Awards—where the Foos were nominated for five awards, including Record of the Year, Album of the Year, and Best Rock Song, and picked up Best Hard Rock Performance for *Echoes, Silence, Patience & Grace*'s stirring opener "The Pretender," and their third Best Rock Album award—plus New York's Madison Square Garden and Japan's Zepp Osaka...

Legendary halls, each and every one of them. But *Live Earth* had stirred a hunger in Grohl. He wanted to tread Wembley Stadium's boards again, and not be hurried offstage to make space for the Pussycat Dolls this time. He wanted Foo Fighters to headline Wembley Stadium on their own—a risky ambition, as he freely admitted. What if they couldn't sell tickets? What if the venue proved too big for them to maintain their fans' attention for the full sprawl of a Foo Fighters concert? And what special treats could the band possibly pull out of the bag to match the scale of the stage?

Live Earth was the biggest audience the group had performed in front of and ignited within Grohl a desire to headline Wembley.

Following the logic that if you book it, they will come, Grohl instructed his agents to sign the group up for a show at Wembley Stadium on June 6, 2008, and held his breath to see if the Foo Fighters' starpower would sell enough tickets for the endeavor not to be a money-losing embarrassment. To Grohl's surprise and relief, not only did the June 6 show quickly sell all 86,000 tickets, but a hastily-added second show the following night also sold out.

Grohl's mood, in the days approaching the show, was a cocktail of giddy excitement, understandable anxiety, disbelief that this was really all happening, and a truly Grohl-ian gratitude for the directions his life had taken. "If this all ended tomorrow, I really would be the happiest guy alive," he told *Metal Hammer*. "I'd still be the same guy, sweating my balls off, jamming as hard as I possibly can in some studio somewhere, making music with my friends. But right now we're enjoying every second. Holy fuck, dude! We're headlining at Wembley fuckin' Stadium! Who wouldn't wanna do that?"

A week before the Wembley shows, Grohl found himself at Liverpool's Anfield Stadium, where Paul McCartney was headlining The Liverpool Sound, celebrating his hometown's year as the European Capital of Culture. Following support sets by local heroes The Zutons, Leeds indie band Kaiser Chiefs, and beloved comic Peter Kay, the esteemed former Beatle took the stage with his band for a show that served as an overview of perhaps the most remarkable career in pop, opening with a

Right: On June 6, 2008, the Foo Fighters made Wembley Stadium their own—and did the same again the very next day.

Left: Grohl rubs shoulders with classic rock royalty, rehearsing alongside Sir Paul McCartney before 2008's The Liverpool Sound concert at Anfield Stadium.

cover of Chan Romero's "Hippy Hippy Shake," a Merseybeat cornerstone, before revisiting hits from The Beatles, McCartney's post-Beatles outfit Wings, and his subsequent solo career. For the Wings classic "Band On The Run," McCartney was joined on guitar by Grohl, who scarcely blanched at the song's complex sections and changes before clambering behind the drumkit to hammer away on a blistering version of The Beatles' "Back In The U.S.S.R."

It was another pinch-yourself-in-case-you're-dreaming moment for Grohl, though he was rubbing shoulders with so many of his heroes at the time that he must've been covered in bruises. To jam with a Beatle in the Liverpool sunshine was undeniable proof that Grohl was now regarded as a peer by the stars who'd inspired and influenced him decades before, and was now entering an upper echelon of rock stardom. As the Wembley dates fast approached, he'd need to tap into the confidence such appearances bred, to overcome his anxieties over playing such a vast venue.

"I remember feeling uncomfortable in front of large audiences for the first few years," Grohl remarked later. "There was one festival in particular when we were opening for David Bowie in France in 1996. I was stood on a huge stage, in front of thousands of people, and I felt completely out of place. I lost faith in our music's ability to translate to a huge field full of punters. I just didn't know if it was right. I suppose it was because I thought I had to be a certain type of frontman. I didn't know what to do upfront. I was a drummer and, all of a sudden, I was put in the front. It was frightening. There was only one way to get over it and that was just to say, 'fuck it.' From then on, I didn't worry about it and I haven't since."

Who knows how loudly Grohl exclaimed "Fuck it!" before running onstage for those two Wembley shows? Whatever, it certainly did the trick, as both nights were unalloyed triumphs, with both band and audience amped up by the sense of occasion. "Hey! Hey! Hey! Wembley fucking Stadium!" greeted Grohl, as the group took the stage at 8pm. "Ladies and gentlemen, I love each and every one of you fucking assholes tonight. I used to think this place was big. . .It's fucking massive! I love it."

The concert movie culled from the shows that was released on DVD later that summer attests that Foo Fighters were a band

Left: Lifelong rock 'n' roll devotee Grohl chews the fat with Led Zeppelin's John Paul Jones (left) and Jimmy Page (right) at the 2008 *GQ* Men of the Year Awards.

Echoes, Silence, Patience & Grace

Grammy Award Best Rock Album, 2008
Brit Award Best International Album, 2008

Released: September 25, 2007
Label: Roswell/RCA
Recorded: March—June, 2007
Studio 606 West, Northridge, Los Angeles, California

PERSONNEL:
Dave Grohl: lead vocals, rhythm guitar, acoustic guitar, piano on "Summer's End," "Statues," and "Home"
Nate Mendel: bass
Taylor Hawkins: drums, backing vocals on "Erase/Replace," "Cheer Up, Boys (Your Make Up Is Running)," "The Pretender" and "But, Honestly," piano on "Summer's End"
Chris Shiflett: lead guitar, acoustic guitar, backing vocals on "Cheer Up, Boys (Your Make Up Is Running)," and "Long Road To Ruin"

ADDITIONAL PERSONNEL:
Drew Hester: percussion on "Come Alive," "Let It Die," "Cheer Up, Boys (Your Make Up Is Running)," "Long Road To Ruin," and "Summer's End"
Rami Jaffee: keyboards on "Let It Die," "Erase/Replace," "Long Road To Ruin," "Come Alive," and "But, Honestly," Accordion on "Statues"
Brantley Kearns Jr.: fiddle on "Statues"
Kaki King: acoustic guitar on "Ballad Of The Beaconsfield Miners"
Pat Smear: rhythm guitar on "Let It Die"
The Section Quartet (arranged and conducted by Audrey Riley): strings on "The Pretender," "Statues," "Home" and "Come Alive"
Oliver Allgood: lute on "Long Road To Ruin"
Gil Norton: production

TRACK LISTING:
All tracks written by Dave Grohl, Taylor Hawkins, Nate Mendel, and Chris Shiflett except where noted

1. "The Pretender"
2. "Let It Die"
3. "Erase/Replace"
4. "Long Road To Ruin"
5. "Come Alive"
6. "Stranger Things Have Happened" (Grohl)
7. "Cheer Up, Boys (Your Make Up Is Running)"
8. "Summer's End"
9. "Ballad Of The Beaconsfield Miners" (Grohl)
10. "Statues"
11. "But, Honestly"
12. "Home"

who rose to the challenge of Wembley. They performed from a revolving stage, placed at the center of the hallowed football pitch, with Grohl often haring off down a long catwalk that led deep into the audience, like the one he'd gadded about on at *Live Earth*. Accompanied by the expanded Foo Fighters band—including Smear, Jaffee, Hester, and, replacing an absent Haden, violinist Jessy Green (formerly of alt-country bands Geraldine Fibbers and The Jayhawks)—they blasted through their biggest hits and the highlights of *Echoes, Silence, Patience & Grace* with greater focus and joy than ever before.

The second night, meanwhile, witnessed what was an increasingly regular occurrence at a Foo Fighters show, the classic rock celebrity guest, though this show's guest stars were more impressive than most. A year earlier, the surviving members of Led Zeppelin had reconvened for their first show in over two decades, at a memorial concert for revered Atlantic Records mogul Ahmet Ertegun. In the months since that show, rumors whispered that Zeppelin would soon tour again, and then whispered that they might even record new material together, before sorrowfully rasping that singer Robert Plant wanted none of it, and the group were now dead and buried. So when Foos friend and collaborator John Paul Jones and Zeppelin guitarist Jimmy Page walked onstage for an encore blitz through their hits "Rock 'n' Roll" and "Ramble On" in the company of the Foos, most in the audience realized it was as close as they'd get to seeing Zeppelin perform again.

"Welcome," grinned an ecstatic Dave Grohl, "to the greatest fucking day of my life!"

Foo Fighters, 2011. (L-R) Chris Shiflett, Dave Grohl, Taylor Hawkins, Pat Smear, Nate Mendel

A Matter Of Time

"We'd been working on this cycle of an album every two years for the last fucking fifteen years. We were all exhausted of flying around the world playing shows five nights a week. But more than that, I started thinking, 'Aren't they fucking sick of us yet?'"

DAVE GROHL

As highs go, the Wembley shows would take some beating. Indeed, when *Q* magazine interviewed Dave shortly beforehand, there was a sense that a paradigm was shifting, that the Foo Fighters might have to come up with some new aims and ambitions after those June shows. As Grohl himself asked, "So what the fuck do we do after two nights at Wembley?"

The immediate answer was, obviously, get into the studio and start demoing new material. As was their habit, the band had been working up some new songs and ideas at soundchecks during the touring for *Echoes, Silence, Patience & Grace*—indeed, Grohl later revealed that the tour had obeyed "a no-soundchecking-songs-we-already-know policy." In the fall of 2008, after a final dash of US shows, the group entered Grandmaster Recorders in Hollywood, where Dave had laid down his replacement drum parts for *The Colour and the Shape* over a decade before, to put these ideas to tape, "rather than just forgetting about them or letting them sit around until we were ready to make another album," as Grohl explained. "Then I had this idea that we should just release an album of all new stuff but just not do anything for it: not go on the road, not make a big deal about it, just record the music and release it. But it didn't feel like it was ready, and we wouldn't be able to just sit around at home if we had a new album, so rather than jump into another cycle of things, it felt like a good idea to stop."

"We didn't want to overstay our welcome in people's faces," added Hawkins. "It just felt like maybe people needed a break from us, too."

The new songs were put on ice, and the Foos agreed upon a short hiatus. Since Grohl's contentious forays with Queens of the Stone Age, the Foo Fighters had agreed as a unit to respect each member's need to make music outside of the group, and so, with this fallow time scheduled, the four members branched off to pursue their extra-curricular activities. Nate Mendel reconnected with his former bandmates in Sunny Day Real Estate, whose earlier reunion—the one Mendel almost quit the Foos for—fell apart after their well-received comeback

Right: 2009 saw Sunny Day Real Estate reunite—this time, without threatening the ongoing future of Nate Mendel's day job, the Foo Fighters.

Left: Taylor Hawkins (right) and his Coattail Riders enjoy a guest appearance from Queen's Roger Taylor (center) and Brian May (left) at a 2010 gig at London's Scala.

Below: Roger Taylor and Brian May also guested on the Coattail Riders' second album, *Red Light Fever*, along with Eliot Easton of The Cars, and one Dave Grohl.

"We didn't want to overstay our welcome in people's faces. It just felt like maybe people needed a break from us, too."

TAYLOR HAWKINS

album *The Rising Tide* was undone by the meager finances of their label, Time Bomb. Jeremy Enigk and William Goldsmith subsequently formed a new band, The Fire Theft, fielding contributions from Mendel when his Foos schedule allowed. But it wasn't until the fall of 2009 that the group's original line-up joined forces again, for a tour of the US and Canada, then Australia and Europe, promoting reissues of their first two albums. Sunny Day Real Estate performed a new song, "10," at these reunion shows, but nothing came of rumors that the band would cut another album together.

Taylor Hawkins ducked out to record a second album with his side-project Taylor Hawkins and the Coattail Riders, *Red Light Fever,* four years after their eponymous debut. While that first album wore its passion for classic rock literally on its sleeve—the cover was an homage to the second album by Ohioan heavy rockers the James Gang—*Red Light Fever* made Hawkins's passion for the classic rock canon even more explicit, fielding guest appearances from Queen's Brian May and Roger Taylor, and Eliot Easton, guitarist with The Cars, while some unknown bum called Dave Grohl also contributed rhythm guitar and backing vocals.

Chris Shiflett, meanwhile, had always kept his dance card full during Foos downtime, maintaining his membership of all-star punk rock comedy covers band Me First and the Gimme Gimmes (also featuring members of NOFX and Lagwagon). He also played in The Real McCoy (fronted by ex-Hanoi Rocks singer Andy McCoy), and recorded two albums with his own punk group Jackson United, which featured his older brother Scott on bass and, on their final album, 2008's *Harmony and Dissonance,* Dave Grohl and Taylor Hawkins on drums. Following Jackson United's hiatus, however, Shiflett changed tack and formed a new group, Chris Shiflett & the Dead Peasants, paying tribute to his love for Americana and cow-punk, whose self-titled debut album surfaced in the summer of 2010.

Unsurprisingly, Grohl also kept busy, not least welcoming a second daughter, Harper Willow, into the world on April 17, 2009. He'd spent the months approaching her birth working on his latest high-profile collaboration, joining forces with old Queens of the Stone Age mucker Josh Homme for new band Them Crooked Vultures, with bass and keys performed by Led Zeppelin legend and occasional Foo Fighters guest musician John Paul Jones. The project had been a long time coming, Grohl first revealing its existence in 2005. "I think the next project that I'm trying to initiate involves me on drums, Josh from Queens of the Stone Age on guitar, and John Paul Jones playing bass," he told me, barely able to hold back his excitement. "That's the next album. That wouldn't suck."

Indeed, it didn't. Recorded throughout the first eight months of 2009 at Homme's Pink Duck Studios in Burbank—which Homme himself described as resembling "a bordello from the cowboy days"—the thirteen-track LP played to the baser end of Queens of the Stone Age's range, tapping the more lascivious corners of Zeppelin's back catalog for inspiration. The band members had indeed mooted this collaboration back in 2005, the project held up by their day-job commitments: first the Foos, then Queens of the Stone Age, and then, finally, Zeppelin's rumored (and then canceled) reunion. Once Robert Plant signaled his distaste for returning to the band that made his name, John Paul Jones called Homme and Grohl and set their long-delayed plans in motion.

Stepping back behind the kit again to record with an actual member of Led Zeppelin was, said Grohl, "the most exciting thing I've done in my whole entire life," though it wasn't without its challenges. "There was a song where what Josh was asking me to do seemed particularly impossible," Grohl told *Kerrang!*'s James McMahon, "and I got so fucking mad and frustrated. But anytime you challenge a musician and get them to that place where they say, 'That's just not what I do,' that's when you start to get the good shit. Josh always fucking pushes me to that place. By the end of the day I'm like, 'I love you, man.'"

The group toured a bunch, making their debut at Chicago's Metro in the summer of 2009, before playing festivals around the globe, playing as support to Arctic Monkeys, and undertaking several tours of their own. Drumming with Them Crooked Vultures, Grohl later confessed, made him feel "like a king." But following their set at the Fuji Rock Festival in July 2010, and despite enduring rumors that a second album was in the offing (schedules permitting, it might still happen), the project went on hiatus. The reason was a familiar one: after having had a fling with another band, Grohl was again missing the comforts of home, and his main squeeze. It was time to make another Foo Fighters album.

A Matter Of Time

Above: Chris Shiflett (center) onstage with his country-tinged side-project the Dead Peasants.

Right: Shiflett returns (briefly) to the ranks of beloved hardcore covers band Me First and the Gimme Gimmes at the 2009 Pinkpop Festival, Netherlands.

When sessions began for what would become *Wasting Light*, Foo Fighters' seventh studio full-length, over three years had elapsed since they had downed tools on *Echoes, Silence, Patience & Grace*—pretty much a lifetime for a band who'd been so solidly prolific. "We'd been working on this cycle of an album every two years for the last fucking fifteen years," remembered Grohl to *NME*. "We were all exhausted of flying around the world playing shows five nights a week. But more than that, I started thinking, 'Aren't they fucking sick of us yet?'"

The reception enjoyed by *Greatest Hits* released in the fall of 2009 had suggested otherwise, selling 4xPlatinum in the UK and reaching number eleven on *Billboard* in the US, as well as topping charts elsewhere in the world. Grohl wasn't hugely enthused at the thought of releasing such a compilation—"It still seems premature, because we're still a functioning, active band," he told BBC Radio 1's Chris Moyles, adding, "these things can seem like an obituary"—but the release offered an opportunity to air a couple of new tracks they'd written on the *Echoes, Silence, Patience & Grace* tour.

And if the solidly melodic, Tom Petty-sounding "Wheels" didn't quite match the caliber of the hits it rubbed shoulders with, "Word Forward" offered more substance. It was written partly in tribute to Grohl's best friend, Jimmy Swanson, who had passed away following a drug overdose in 2008. "I'd known him since we were six years old," Grohl told the audience of *VH1 Storytellers* in 2009. "We shared everything together—we discovered music together, we discovered weed together, we discovered punk rock and underground metal. We were brothers. And when he passed away, it had such a profound impact on me. . .I realized, 'Wow, that part of my life is over.' And now there's only one way to go; you just have to move on."

The track was bittersweet, elegiac, but, in a classic Grohling flourish, ultimately uplifting—Dave musing over his loss, but reasoning ultimately that his life must go on, moving forwards. A simple message, but totally convincing when delivered by an artist whose rock transcended artifice, whose sincerity could electrify. But if the song threw an ultimately life-affirming light upon a tragedy, Grohl wasn't done brooding over the loss. It would ultimately inspire one of his greatest songs.

Work on *Wasting Light* began in September 2010, Grohl having chosen as producer an important figure from his past: Butch Vig, the man who had produced Nirvana's breakthrough album, *Nevermind*, almost two decades earlier. Rather than record the album at Studio 606 West, Grohl had more intimate environs in mind—the garage of his family home. "We have this really casual disregard for the outside world," grinned Grohl to *Rock Sound*'s Jonathan Horsley. "We stay away from things that feel contrived, from things that seem too unrealistic. The making of this album, in a garage, was a terrific way to represent our band."

Terrific the scheme may have been, but it presented some challenges for Vig. "First Dave said, 'I want to do it in my garage,'" the producer laughed. "Then he dropped the bombshell: 'I don't want to use any computers. No Pro Tools. All tape. I want to record, mix and master off tape.' That's how I learned to make records, but I haven't done that process in fifteen years. Okay. . .you guys have to be able to play it really, really well! We can fix everything in Pro Tools—you can take a band that's not very good and make them razor tight. It's an amazing tool. But this became more about the band's performances. Working with Pro Tools, it's not challenging. They were up for a challenge."

Opposite: At the 2009 MusiCares Person of the Year Award, to honor Neil Diamond, Grohl and Jordyn Blum drop clues that their family might soon welcome another member.

Right: *Chris Shiflett & the Dead Peasants*. The 2010 album marked the debut on vinyl of the guitarist's second side-project.

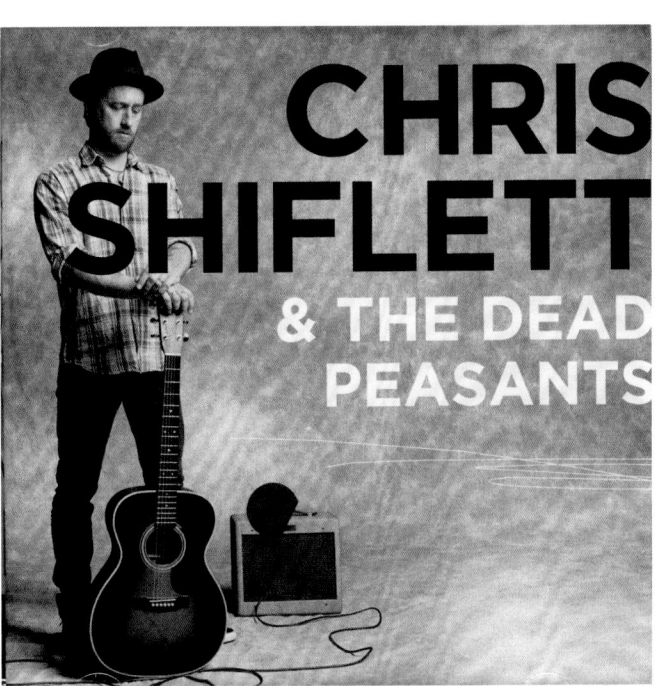

They were also up for rocking hard. The last couple of Foo Fighters albums had been experimental, exercises in stretching the boundaries of their music, expanding their frame of reference. Strings, bossa nova, acoustic concerts, unflinching name-dropping of Steely Dan: all bets were off. This time round, however, the Foos were hungry for more immediate, visceral pleasures. "Back when we made *There Is*

Them Crooked Vultures, 2010. (L-R) John Paul Jones, Dave Grohl, Josh Homme

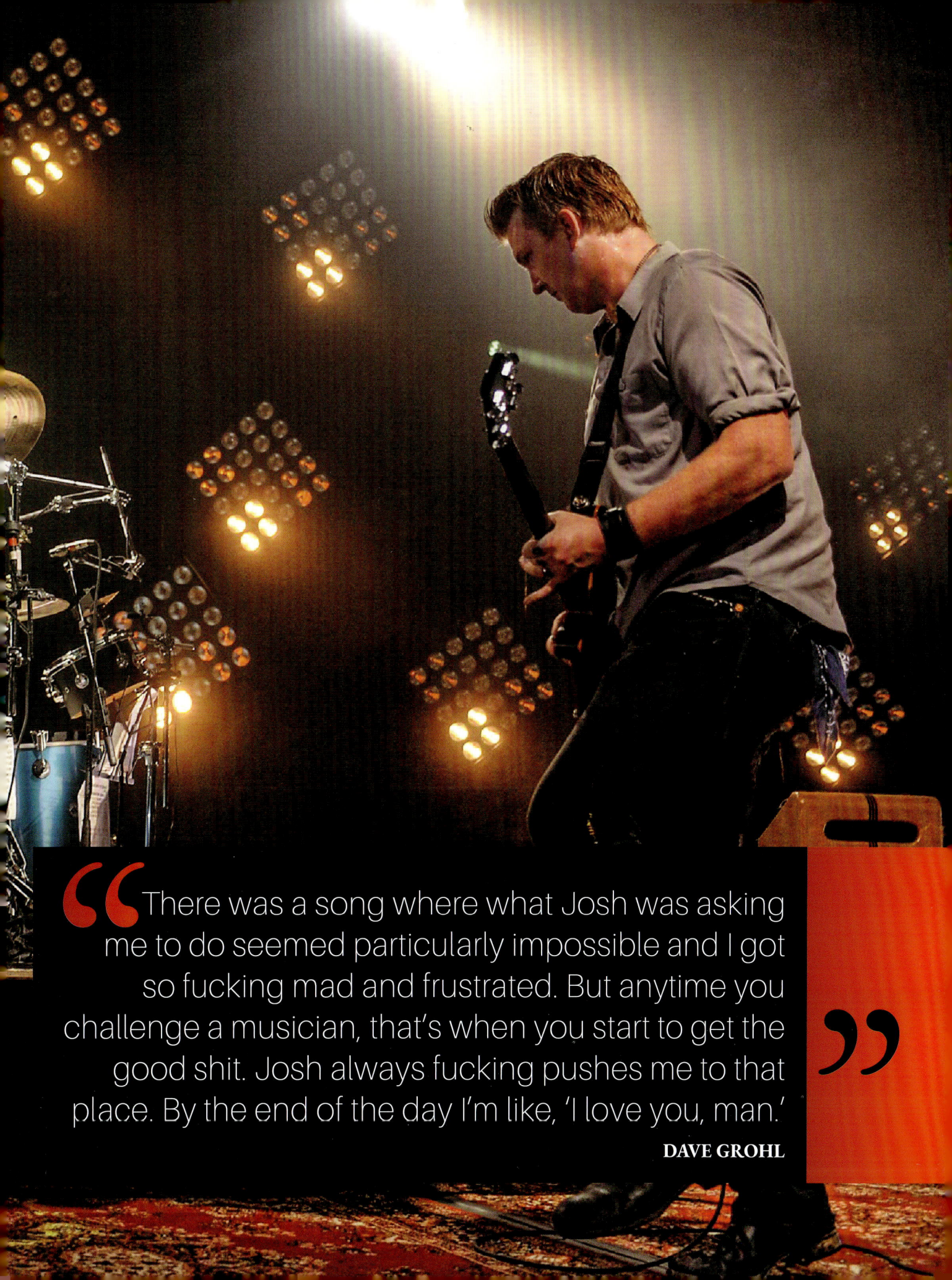

> "There was a song where what Josh was asking me to do seemed particularly impossible and I got so fucking mad and frustrated. But anytime you challenge a musician, that's when you start to get the good shit. Josh always fucking pushes me to that place. By the end of the day I'm like, 'I love you, man.'
> **DAVE GROHL**

Nothing Left to Lose, we really focused on melody," Grohl told *Guitar World*. "At the time, music was going through the nu-metal shift, and it was all screaming choruses with distortion pedals and creepy, quiet verses. It was all really in your face and brash. So for the last ten years, we tried to get more mellow and melodic. But the idea of making this record in a garage with analog equipment and Butch Vig…it only made sense to make a big fuckin' rock record."

Left: Released fifteen years after their debut album was recorded, Foo Fighters' 2010 *Greatest Hits* album wasn't Grohl's idea, but was a smash hit.

Opposite: Jimmy Swanson, pictured here with Jordyn and Violet Maye, was one of Grohl's oldest, dearest friends. His death inspired the song "I Should Have Known."

This mindset gave full reign to a more primal Foo Fighters than we'd heard since "All My Life." Opener "Burning Bridge" began with a salutary thrashy guitar-and-drums tattoo, Grohl's howl of "These are my famous last words!" and getting metallic like prime Helmet, before adding just enough melody for lift-off. "Rope," one of the few surviving tunes from the post-*Echoes* tour sessions, took a hook-drenched clever pop song and dressed it in barbs and razor blades. "White Limo," trailed by a fantastically grindhouse promo video that featured Lemmy himself, driving the titular vehicle around Los Angeles with the Foos partying hard in the back, barked and screamed like banshee heavy metal. If their recent albums had aimed high and wide, much of *Wasting Light* was directed at the mosh-pit, perfect for slam-dancing and stage-diving. "Those songs could have been Dain Bramage songs, the band I was in when I was seventeen," Grohl said, and he meant it as a good thing. Garage punk rock, recorded in an actual garage.

One of Grohl's greatest punk influences had been early-eighties Minneapolis trio Hüsker Dü, whose emotionally searing, lightning-fast, phosphorescent pop had helped draw the blueprint for the metallicized melodies that took Nirvana overground. Grohl had finally met that band's former singer and guitarist Bob Mould at a thirtieth anniversary celebration for legendary Washington, D.C. punk venue The 9:30 Club, and told Mould he considered him a hero. The duo hit it off and exchanged numbers, and Grohl invited him down to his garage to lend guitars and vocals to the molten folk-rock of "Dear Rosemary," whose scoured tunefulness could have fallen off of one of Mould's latterday solo albums. "He, of course, is a brilliant songwriter and an excellent musician," remembered Grohl. "But to have Bob in my house, hanging out with my children, playing a song we are collaborating on for my record, was just huge for me."

If *Wasting Light*'s devil-horns-throwing slam-dance wasn't dragged down by any soft rock power ballads this time round, that didn't mean the album didn't carry any weight. "I Should Have Known" was raw, its slow rumble rueful and full of regret, Grohl's vocal performance among the greatest of his career. "At the end of that take, the hair on my neck stood up," Vig later recalled. "I couldn't say anything. Dave looked like he was crying, because he was singing so hard. He was obviously channeling something inside."

Grohl had begun writing the song about Jimmy Swanson, but as it developed, he began to realize it could be about his friendship with Kurt, too; certainly, there were parallels. "I should have known it would end this way," Grohl laments in the opening line. Later, he's howling, "I cannot forgive you yet, You leave my heart in debt." "'I Should Have Known' is about all the people I've lost," Dave would later explain, "not just Kurt."

The song was underpinned by a remarkable performance by the Foos, especially Hawkins's colossal, tumble-down drum fills, and a soaring bassline courtesy of guest four-stringer Krist Novoselic. The track reunited Grohl, Novoselic, and Vig in the studio for the first time since *Nevermind*. "It was intense," admitted Vig. "Dave opens a bottle of wine, a friend had sent me a bottle of bootleg whiskey. We start sipping on that, and just sat down and told stories. We were up until about two in the morning. It was powerful—all those memories came flooding back."

Left: One of Grohl's greatest heroes, singer and guitarist Bob Mould, guest-starred on the Foo Fighters' seventh album, *Wasting Light*.

Above: Mould's first band, Hüsker Dü - who also featured singing drummer Grant Hart (center) and bassist Greg Norton (left)—were one of hardcore's most influential groups.

Novoselic wasn't the only former Nirvana member present for the sessions; *Wasting Light* saw the return of Pat Smear to full-time Foo Fighter duty, following three or so years as a touring sideman. "I'd wanted to do nothing, really," Smear told the *National Post*, of his reasons for quitting the group years before. "And I accomplished it for a really long time. But then I started missing it. Every time a new record would come out, I would really miss it and be like, 'Aw, I wish I'd played on that.' That's how it started."

There was a stability to Foo Fighters that Pat appreciated, the antithesis of all the bands he'd been in before. "It's a band of people with non-destructive tendencies," he laughed. "That band where everybody shows up on time and does their job and there's no drug addicts and no crazies, and it's kind of awesome. I love it."

In addition to recording an album at home, Grohl also greenlit the making of a biographical documentary about the band, Oscar-winner James Moll's *Foo Fighters: Back and Forth*. Grohl had only intended the movie to cover the making of *Wasting Light* at first, but then the project snowballed into something bigger: a feature-length, no-holds-barred history of the group, which doubled up as a therapy session for its members. Every twist in the band's career was covered, from

> "It's a band of people with non-destructive tendencies. That band where everybody shows up on time and does their job and there's no drug addicts and no crazies, and it's kind of awesome. I love it."
> **PAT SMEAR**

Pat Smear shares the stage with Krist Novoselic once again, as Grohl's all-star Sound City Players perform at the Hollywood Palladium, 2012.

Above: Director James Moll (center) gave the band—and its ex-members—a chance to reflect on their extraordinary story in 2011's *Foo Fighters: Back and Forth*.

Dave's crawling from the wreckage of Nirvana to cut the first album, to the grueling making of *The Colour and the Shape*, to losing William Goldsmith, and then Pat Smear, and then Franz Stahl, and then, almost, Nate, to Taylor's overdose, and Grohl's seduction to Queens of the Stone Age's dark side. Moll interviewed the whole band, and also Goldsmith and Stahl, both still nursing the wounds from their exit from the group.

It made for intense and not always easy viewing, doubly so if that was your story being told onscreen. The interviews made Grohl reconsider the circumstances under which the former members had left the group, and saw Mendel and Grohl confront for the first time Nate's enduring loyalties towards his former Sunny Day Real Estate bandmates, while also revealing to Hawkins that he had inspired *In Your Honor*'s

Wasting Light

Grammy Award Best Rock Album, 2011

Released: April 12, 2011
Label: Roswell/RCA
Recorded: September 6–December 21, 2010
Dave Grohl's garage

PERSONNEL:
Dave Grohl: lead vocals, rhythm guitar, lead guitar on "White Limo"
Pat Smear: rhythm guitar, lead guitar, baritone guitar
Nate Mendel: bass
Taylor Hawkins: drums, backing vocals, percussion
Chris Shiflett: lead guitar, backing vocals, tenor guitar, rhythm guitar on "White Limo"

Additional personnel:
Bob Mould: guitar and backing vocals on "Dear Rosemary," backing vocals on "I Should Have Known"
Krist Novoselic: bass and accordion on "I Should Have Known"
Rami Jaffee: keyboards on "Bridge Burning" and "Rope," Mellotron on "I Should Have Known," organ on "Walk" and "Dear Rosemary"
Jessy Greene: violin on "I Should Have Known"
Fee Waybill: backing vocals on "Miss The Misery"
Butch Vig: production, percussion on "Back & Forth"
Drew Hester: percussion on "Arlandria," hidden cowbell strike on "Rope"

TRACK LISTING:
All tracks written by Dave Grohl, Taylor Hawkins, Nate Mendel, Chris Shiflett, and Pat Smear

1. "Bridge Burning"
2. "Rope"
3. "Dear Rosemary"
4. "White Limo"
5. "Arlandria"
6. "These Days"
7. "Back & Forth"
8. "A Matter Of Time"
9. "Miss The Misery"
10. "I Should Have Known"
11. "Walk"

"On The Mend." "After the movie we all looked at each other," remembered Grohl, "and it was strange. To think that I've spent so much of my life with Pat, I've spent sixteen years with Nate, and gone through so much shit with Taylor over the last fourteen years. And we're still happy, and it still works."

"It hasn't all been fun," Grohl admitted to *NME*. "We've had moments when we didn't want to be a band anymore, we've had moments when we didn't know if we were gonna survive. We've had some great victories, and we've had some really lousy shit happen. James got us to say things we might not even say to each other."

Moll's film dug into the messy maw of the band and their relationships with each other, but its overall message was of a group of friends, a bond that transcended the tensions and challenges they faced, and a shared mission that just seemed to grow more focused as the year's passed. Yeah, they'd gone through shit, but this didn't shake their resolve to go through more, if their journey demanded it. *Wasting Light* closed out with "Walk," as naked a statement of intent as they'd yet managed, Grohl's essential optimism and faith rendered purely in words and music, as he howled, over stomping, rising power chords, "I never wanna die! I never wanna leave! I'll never say goodbye!"

It was the anthem of a lifer, just like Mike Watt had been for years, just like Dave Grohl was now. He'd released a greatest hits, had a movie made about his band, but Grohl was in no mood for obituaries or endings: his journey still had miles to go, and some of his most ambitious projects still lay before him.

> "It hasn't all been fun. We've had moments when we didn't want to be a band anymore, we've had moments when we didn't know if we were gonna survive. We've had some great victories, and we've had some really lousy shit happen."
>
> **DAVE GROHL**

Foo Fighters, 2011, Toronto, Canada. (L-R) Dave Grohl, Nate Mendel, Taylor Hawkins, Chris Shiflett, Pat Smear

Foo Fighters: *Sonic Highways* New York premiere, Ed Sullivan Theater, October 14, 2014. (L-R) Rami Jaffee, Nate Mendel, Taylor Hawkins, Dave Grohl, Chris Shiflett, and Pat Smear

Congregations

"We're all connected by something—maybe it's a river that runs underground, maybe it's Woody Guthrie, maybe it's Chuck D, whatever….That conversation became my goal. I want to talk about these people, I want to talk about music. But I want to get to this. I want this to be the conversation point."

DAVE GROHL

Seven albums into the Foo Fighters' career, Dave Grohl was on a mission to keep things interesting. When it came time to take *Wasting Light* on the road, he was reluctant to jump into the usual grind of US-tour/European-festivals/world-tour that had followed every other Foo Fighters release. Production of the album had shaken up the typical Foos pattern—moving recording into his garage, reconnecting Grohl with Vig and Novoselic—and while the itinerary would eventually take in the open-air shindigs and enormodomes the Foos usually played, Grohl was again possessed by a desire to disrupt the typical order of things.

Their first unexpected gesture was to celebrate the final night of work on *Wasting Light* with a surprise gig at Paladinos, a little rock bar in the LA suburb of Tarzana; the show was agreeably chaotic, with the group debuting four songs from the new album that night. Next, following a slew of similar small sneak-previews across Europe and Australia, the group set off for the first leg of their American tour, holding a competition whereby eight winners would get to host a Foo Fighters concert in their own garage. Contestants had to submit a photograph of their garage and the reason, in twenty-five words or less, why the Foos should play there. The concerts included a jam in the carport of a retired New York fireman injured during the 9/11 attacks, a hoedown in a Washington, D.C. farmhouse, a concert for a super-fan in Toronto who got to play guitar with the group ("After 16 years, the Foo Fighters finally have four fucking guitarists," grinned Grohl), and a stomping set in a Chicago rec room. "The big arena shows are fun," Grohl said to one winner, "but they are not as memorable as this."

Even after the garage shows, when the group knuckled down to the hard work of taking the new album to the people across the world, the Foos embraced every opportunity to break from the routine and keep things fresh. Like on September 16, 2011, when the Foos swung into Kansas City to play at the Spirit Center, only to find the members of the Westboro Baptist Church—notorious for their homophobia, transphobia, and attacks on other religions—protesting outside the venue, toting banners proclaiming "God hates fags" and "God loves dead soldiers," along with amateurish photoshopped images proclaiming

Left: Producer Butch Vig (right) with the surviving members of Nirvana, twenty years on from their landmark album, *Nevermind*.

Obama the anti-Christ. The Foos responded by arriving at the venue on the back of a flatbed truck before the show, dressed up as plaid-clad hicks and rednecks, in fake beards, mustaches, and, in Nate Mendel's case, Willie Nelson-esque ponytail.

The boys had previously sported these costumes earlier that year for *Hot Buns*, a hilarious viral video promoting the *Wasting Light* North American tour, starring the Foos as truckers indulging in a naked dance routine to Queen's homoerotic classic, "Body Language." This afternoon, the flatbed truck pulled up alongside the protesters while the band performed "Keep It Clean," a parody country song that included lines like "I think I'm in the mood for some hot-man muffins," and "Rubbin' and a-lovin' and a-scrubbing' and a-truckin' / Maybe, if we're lucky, just a little bear-huggin'" (The tune even raised a reluctant smile from some of the creepy protesters, and, from Shirley Phelps-Roper, daughter of church founder Fred Phelps, an admission that she "loved that song.") As the flatbed truck pulled away, the scoreboard should have read, "Foo Fighters: 1, Creepy Bigots: 0."

Grohl's extra-curricular activities also helped keep life as a Foo Fighter from getting too samey, and in 2011 he started work on an ambitious scheme: directing his first feature-length documentary. The project was inspired while Grohl was setting up his garage studio to record *Wasting Light*; as he was trying to track down the vintage equipment he needed to get the sessions down on analog tape, Butch Vig suggested he contact legendary Los Angeles recording studio Sound City, as it had hit hard times, and was selling off some of its gear.

"The studio is part of my life," Grohl later explained. "I don't know if I'd be here if it wasn't for that studio." Sound City was where Nirvana had recorded *Nevermind*, with Butch Vig, in 1991; it wasn't as plush as the more upmarket and fancy studios megastars were beginning to frequent in the nineties, but it was perfect for the trio. "We basically slept in a van when we were on tour, so we weren't used to top-of-the-line shit," Grohl remembered to *Kerrang!*'s Simon Young. "Sound City was kinda run-down, and was a perfect match for us."

Sound City might have lost some of its luster by the time Nirvana arrived to record their epochal album, but it had an impressive history. After opening its doors in 1969, the following year the studio hosted Neil Young, then recording *After the Gold Rush*. In the ensuing years, it hosted Elton John, Fleetwood Mac, and Cheap Trick, and, following *Nevermind*, the likes of Kyuss, Red Hot Chili Peppers, and Queens of the Stone Age turned up for a little of its magic. One of the studio's great attractions was its array of classic recording equipment. "I said if they ever wanted to get rid of the Neve 8028 board in the A room, to let me know," Grohl said. "They were like, 'I'd sell my grandmother before I'd sell that board.' Okay, just saying. It was only a matter of time before they closed, and they asked me if I was serious about buying the console."

Right: Dressed down in hillbilly gear and fake beards, the Foo Fighters make the bigoted Westboro Baptist Church look like fools.

Grohl had the board installed at Studio 606 West—"It was stressful as it hadn't moved in forty years," Grohl said. "It was like robbing a tomb or something"—and was moved enough by the studio's history, a statement on a music industry in transition in the digital age, to commemorate Sound City's story on celluloid. He'd never made a movie before, but then nobody had ever taught him to drum, and no one had shown him how to make an album before he recorded the Foo Fighters' debut, all by himself, in a week. Grohl had always been an autodidact, and so it was when he started directing pictures. "I don't know how to make movies, but I could tell you the story of Sound City like that [snaps fingers]," Grohl told Simon Young. "So why would I need anyone's help? We rounded up the coolest people we knew, and it was fucking great."

Grohl's movie told the story of the studio, from its opening to its eventual closure, talking to the artists who recorded there, and even interviewing Rupert Neve, the eighty-six-year-old engineer who had designed the Neve sound board Grohl had been salivating over (there were only three others in existence). It also covered the installation of the Neve board at Studio 606 West and, to celebrate its arrival, Grohl invited a number of high-profile former Sound City clients to jam with him and

"I wasn't making it [*Sound City*] so people would think I was a great director. The intention of that movie was to inspire people to love the human element of music, or go out and start a band."

DAVE GROHL

christen his new piece of gear. His recent collaborations with the likes of Paul McCartney, Brian May, and Roger Taylor had obviously given Grohl a feel for working with classic rock superstars. The sessions filmed for the movie (and later released as soundtrack album *Sound City: Real to Reel*) saw Grohl and his Foo Fighters playing with the likes of McCartney, Stevie Nicks (on "You Can't Fix This," originally written for *In Your Honor*) and Cheap Trick's Rick Nielsen, as well as longtime friends Trent Reznor (Grohl had drummed on Nine Inch Nails' 2005 album *With Teeth*), Josh Homme, and Krist Novoselic. On December 12, 2012 at Madison Square Garden, Grohl played drums behind Novoselic and Pat Smear, with Paul McCartney on vocals, for the Concert for Sandy Relief, a benefit to aid victims of Hurricane Sandy that also starred Bruce Springsteen, The Who and The Rolling Stones. The supergroup performed their track "Cut Me Some Slack" from the *Sound City* soundtrack during McCartney's segment, and then reprised the song a week later on *Saturday Night Live*. An expanded version of the Sound City Players, sans McCartney, went on to perform at the Sundance Film Festival in January 2013, followed by appearances on the late-night chat shows, and a climactic appearance at that March's South by Southwest festival, to coincide with the soundtrack's release.

Above: Novoselic and Grohl back Sir Paul McCartney at the 12-12-12 concert, benefiting victims of Hurricane Sandy.

Right: To promote his documentary, *Sound City*, Grohl shares the limelight with Rupert Neve, designer of the console on which *Nevermind* was recorded.

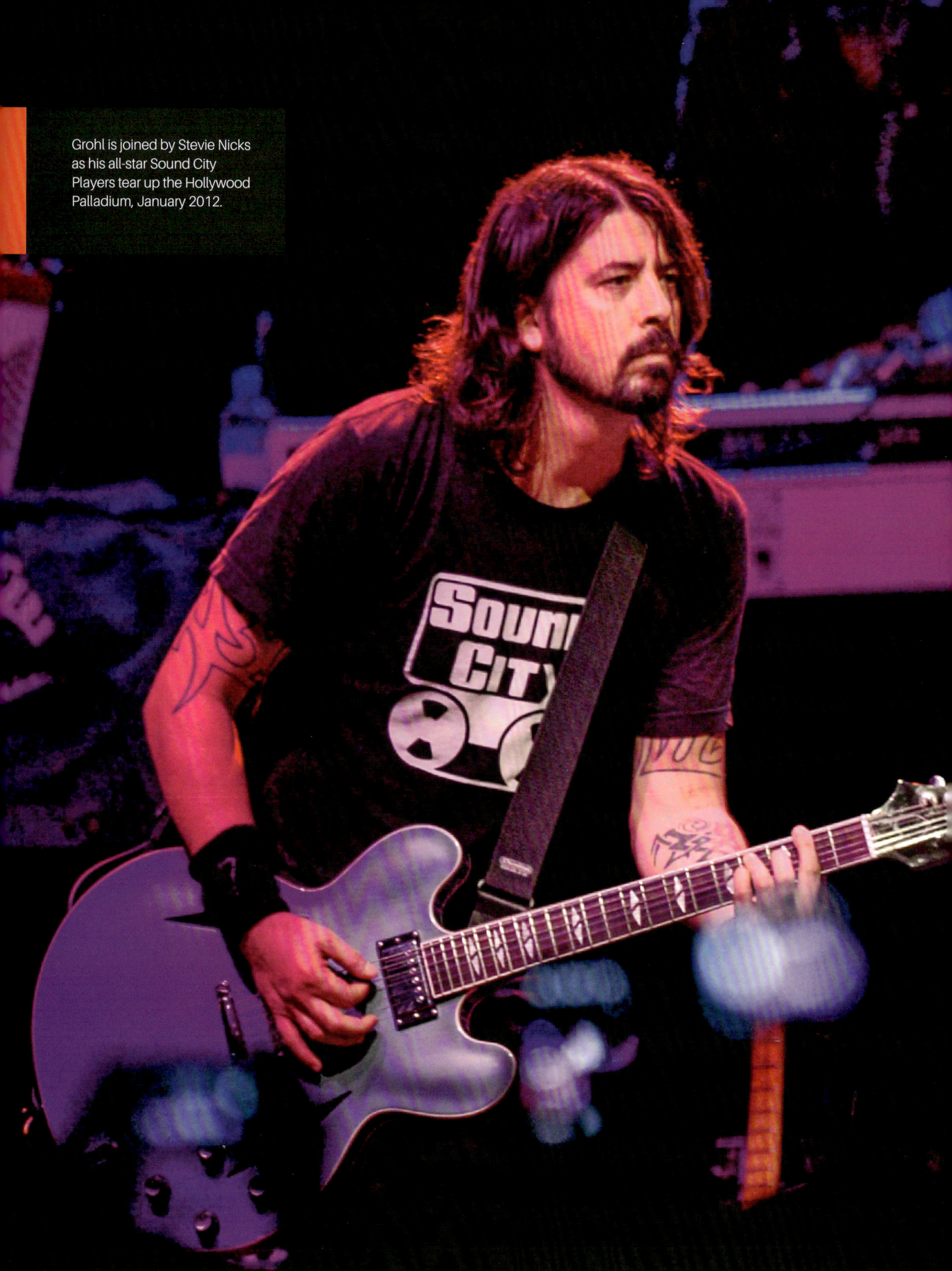

Grohl is joined by Stevie Nicks as his all-star Sound City Players tear up the Hollywood Palladium, January 2012.

Grohl later said he didn't make the movie to win critical acclaim: "I wasn't making it so people would think I was a great director," he told Simon Young. "The intention of that movie was to inspire people to love the human element of music, or go out and start a band." But *Sound City* went on to enjoy widespread praise, and Grohl's taste of life behind the camera would prove a key influence on the Foo Fighters' next album, and their most ambitious project to date: an eight-part HBO documentary series that would secure Grohl a sit-down chat with the President of the United States.

It was that theme of "inspiring people to love the human element of music" that coursed throughout *Sonic Highways*, the eighth Foo Fighters studio album, recorded at eight studios across America while Grohl was filming the documentary series of the same name. Produced for cable channel HBO, the series followed Grohl and his Foos as they criss-crossed America, in search of inspiration for their new album and, on a grander scale, tracing the story of American popular music. With Butch Vig in tow, the group cut a track per episode, inspired by the stories of the cities they visited, the key figures Grohl interviewed, and the paths they crossed.

Right: Steve Albini in his famed Chicago recording studio, Electrical, both guest stars in Grohl's rockumentary series, *Sonic Highways*.

Left: Taylor Hawkins plays cheerleader as another rock legend, Cheap Trick guitarist Rick Nielsen, joins the Sound City Players at New York's Hammerstein Ballroom.

An ambitious project. But Grohl's initial scheme was even grander. "Originally, it was going to be global," he told me. "I'd go to places people don't know much about, like Reykjavik, go talk about music there, and how their culture has influenced the music there, or to São Paulo, exploring the origins of Brazilian rhythm and how that influenced a band like Sepultura. But it was just too much. So we zeroed in on America, because America's a big place—different accents, different cultures, different histories and different kinds of music. Everything's interconnected now, but there used to be isolation, and that isolation developed communities that eventually formed something specific. That's what I thought was really interesting. Like, how did Chicago get the Blues? Chicago's about as far north as you can get, but the blues was based in the [Mississippi] Delta. And what I learned was cultural and historic—following the emancipation of the slaves, millions of African-Americans moved North to get work, and brought their music with them to Chicago. And the city influenced the sound. They weren't sitting in a field with a guitar anymore, now they were in a club with a little amp, and people were dancing and drinking. So the show's concept was, 'How does the environment influence the music?' Not just the room you record in. . .what it is about that city that influences the music you make there?"

"Of course you meet assholes every now and then. But most of the time, if you walk backstage at a music festival, and there's six guys sitting around the table with a bottle of whiskey, those are the guys you want to hang out with. Because they actually dig it."

DAVE GROHL

The roots of the project, Grohl said, lay in conversations he'd had with fellow musicians during his years on the road. "One of my favorite things about what I do is that I get to travel around and talk to people about music…of course, there are times when you're jamming with some iconic legend and it dawns on you that you're in the same room together, and you get butterflies and your knees start to wobble a little. But when a musician sits down with another musician and you talk about music, it's just the same as it would be in the back of a tour bus, or belly-up to the bar, or backstage at a music festival. I was always the guy who would turn up to the festival early, grab a bottle of whiskey and start knocking on dressing room doors, to see like who was gonna be the other guy who wanted to talk. And I would always find one. And over the years I've met so many people that way that when it comes time to do something like this, I just email them and say, 'Hey, I'm doing a project, can I talk to you?' Most musicians are pretty fuckin' cool, because they get to do what they want to do. Of course you meet assholes every now and then. But most of the time, if you walk backstage at a music festival, and there's six guys sitting around the table with a bottle of whiskey, those are the guys you want to hang out with. Because they actually dig it."

Congregations

Opposite: *Sonic Highways* told the story of some of Grohl's formative influences, including hardcore legends Bad Brains.

Right: *Sonic Highways* didn't just concentrate on punk legends. Country hero Willie Nelson and ZZ Top's Billy Gibbons were also key interviewees.

The show started out in Chicago, where Grohl's exploration of the city's blues roots still left time for a chat with Big Black and Shellac frontman and legendary producer Steve Albini, and Cheap Trick's Rick Nielsen, who lent guest guitars to the track they recorded at Albini's Electrical Audio. From there, they visited Washington, D.C. to learn about go-go music, and receive a quick lesson in the home-grown hardcore scene via local heroes (Fugazi, Minor Threat) and Bad Brains' Darryl Jenifer and Dr. Know. And Grohl's former Scream bandmates Pete Stahl and Skeeter Thompson helped the band cut the punk rock dash of "The Feast And The Famine" at Inner Ear Studios, where much of the city's hardcore output was recorded. Next, the band traveled to Nashville, Tennessee, talking country with Willie Nelson and Dolly Parton, and Zac Brown, at whose Southern Ground Studio they cut their delicately twangsome "Congregation." Then on to Austin, Texas, to discuss psychedelia with Butthole Surfer Gibby Haynes, The 13th Floor Elevators's Roky Erickson, and ZZ Top's Billy Gibbons, while blues scion Gary Clark Jr. lent guitar to "What Did I Do?/God As My Witness." Then it was on to Los Angeles—a trip that prompts a sentimental journey for Pat Smear as he revisited his days with the Germs, and a hang-out in the desert at Josh Homme's Rancho De La Luna studio, where the Foos cut "Outside" with Eagles and James Gang guitarist Joe Walsh. Then there was a visit to New Orleans, one of America's most historical music cities, chewing the fat with Dr. John, Allen Toussaint, and Cyril Neville, and recording "In The Clear" with the Preservation Hall Jazz Band, who've been playing New Orleans jazz for five decades.

The series ended with a trip to New York, getting to grips with the Big Apple's abundant soundclashes by meeting up with LL Cool J, Public Enemy's Chuck D, Thurston Moore, and Kiss's Paul Stanley, and cutting "I Am A River" at The Magic Shop. But the penultimate episode was perhaps Grohl's

Right: Gibby Haynes, lunatic frontman of the brilliant Butthole Surfers, was another electrifying interviewee.

Opposite: Dolly Parton. Another unlikely guest star in Grohl's heartfelt history of popular music in America.

most heartfelt, returning to Seattle, and recording at Robert Lang Studios. "That studio had such a big impact for me," Grohl says, "Because it was the last place that Nirvana recorded. That's where I did the first Foo Fighters record by myself. To me, that place represents totally starting over." Tooling around Seattle, Grohl hooks up with old friend Barrett Jones and listens back to copious old demos he cut while still in Nirvana, including the comedic hard-rock rutter "The Hooker Song." "I was in a band with a brilliant songwriter, a great singer," Grohl recalled. "Who the fuck cared what I was doing in my time off? It was just fun."

Preserving that sense of fun had become an essential part of the creativity for Grohl, along with maintaining a certain absence of self-consciousness. "The last record was the first where we realized we should just be ourselves and do our own thing," he told me. "For years we tried to open all of these different doors—acoustic records, orchestration, double albums, all that. And I realized if we just stop trying and play music, then we'll play like the Foo Fighters, and it won't be this contrived shift in direction. The restrictions we put ourselves under for this album. . .We had only a short time to record stuff, we were moving to different rooms and building studios. The room we recorded in, in New Orleans, was two-hundred-years-old with no microphones in it, so we had to haul our tape machine to New Orleans and build a control room in the office. . .So we didn't have time to overthink anything. And I liked that."

The album the show sired was an exercise in subtle contradictions. For all the guest stars, peripatetic sessions, and diverse influences, the music of *Sonic Highways* was some of the most archetypal Foo Fighters yet, a soaring, emotive, big-hearted whole that could embrace the D.C.-hardcore-influenced hurtle of "The Feast And The Famine," the unabashed Beatles vamps of the epic "What Did I Do?/With God As My Witness," the ethereal complexity of the Seattle-recorded "Subterranean," and still be of a piece. Lyrically, it was—like the show—both wide in its scope and perhaps more introspective and autobiographical than any Foos album since *The Colour and the Shape*. Not that Dave was venting any domestic turbulence this time around—the Grohl-Blum marriage happier and more stable than ever, third daughter Ophelia Saint arriving on August 1, 2014—but, instead, finding lyrics that engaged in differing degrees of subtlety his enduring passion for music, a channel for his essential optimism, his faith in something larger; not god, but the mortal communities and congregations that surround music scenes, the power of that music. It wasn't all upbeat—"Subterranean" bore a site-specific darkness and melancholy, with Grohl's references to being "mined to Hell and back again"—but, like the show, the songs spoke to Grohl's almost Capra-esque vision of America and its relationship with its music.

Opposite: The story of New Orleans' contribution to American culture, meanwhile, was retold to Grohl by musicians Allen Toussaint, Cyril Neville, and Dr. John.

Left: Roky Erickson, former frontman of garage-psych legends 13th Floor Elevators, helped Grohl explore the musical history of Austin, Texas.

It was a theme clearest in the final episode, and Grohl's interview with Steve Rosenthal, founder and owner of The Magic Shop, who talked about how he and his colleagues had barely weathered tough times after 9/11, and how the studio was struggling and might not survive (in fact it closed in 2016). It was a frank conversation, which spoke to a music industry struggling with hitherto unimaginable challenges, and stalwarts like Rosenthal who were being taken for granted, and who would be missed when they were gone. But there was a beauty to their connection for Grohl, despite the stakes at play in their conversation. "Rather than talk about the color of the knobs on his really awesome Neve board, we wound up talking about America, and how we used to take care of each other," Grohl said on the show. "I looked at my interview with Steve like the message of this entire project. We're all connected by something—maybe it's a river that runs underground, maybe it's Woody Guthrie, maybe it's Chuck D, whatever. . .That conversation became my goal. I want to talk about these people, I want to talk about music. But I want to get to *this*. I want *this* to be the conversation point."

It was a theme warmed to by the show's biggest guest, President Barack Obama, who told Grohl, "It's all about the garage band, the juke joint, the jazz club. It's about people rejecting what's already there, to create something new. That's always been a theme in American popular music and rock 'n' roll: you got a dream, and you take a chance, and you make it. There is a connection, all these different musical rivers that run together to make American music. There's nothing more unifying in this country than our music."

Like Grohl, Obama was also a true believer. Dave had met the president a few times before, playing events at the Kennedy Center and the White House. "He's genuinely a very down-to-earth, easy-going, nice person," Grohl said. "When he walks into a room the first thing he does is try to disarm any nerves you might have because you're meeting the fucking leader of the free world. He calls you by your first name, and then asks you about your kids. He's a human being—it's hard to imagine that he's a guy with an incredibly difficult job.

"I wanted to talk to him about America as a country where the opportunity to follow your dreams is real. Like, someone

Congregations

"It's all about the garage band, the juke joint, the jazz club. There is a connection, all these different musical rivers that run together to make American music. There's nothing more unifying in this country than our music."

BARACK OBAMA

Foo Fighters: The Band That Dave Made

"To this day, when I think of Nirvana, it doesn't seem that different to me to Scream, or Dain Bramage, or Freakbaby or any of the other bands I was in as a kid. Some of them might have gotten platinum albums, some of them might have worked at a furniture warehouse on the weekend, but they're just bands, just people."

DAVE GROHL

Right: Public Enemy's Chuck D and legendary rapper LL Cool J appeared in *Sonic Highways* to piece together the history of hip-hop.

Left: Grohl plays alongside Joe Walsh and Gary Clark Jr. at *The Night That Changed America: A Grammy Salute to The Beatles.*

like Buddy Guy, who built a guitar from wires and nails from his porch screen door, but is now considered a blues legend who has influenced everyone from Hendrix to the Rolling Stones. That all just started with a dream, you know. So I wanted to talk about our country as a place where that could happen. I'm a fucking high school drop-out, and now I'm in the Rock and Roll Hall of Fame, and HBO gave me a TV series, only because I really fucking wanted to do it. And I never took lessons to do any of that, I'm a fucking spaz, but if there's something I want to do, if it's in my brain, I have to do it, I have to complete it. That was the basis of our conversation."

Obama wasn't the first president Grohl had met. "I met Bush and Clinton. And it's funny, because when I met Bush, I was not aligned with his politics at all. I was at the White House for a function, the Who were getting a Kennedy Center Honor and I was asked to play, and someone said, 'Would you like your picture taken with the president?' And I thought, 'I don't really know if I want my picture taken with *this* president.' My wife said, 'C'mon, you have to do it.' So I walked up to him, and he said 'Where you from?' And I said, 'I'm from Virginia, actually, just outside of Washington, D.C., and I'm playing at the Kennedy Center tonight.' Half an hour later, I'm walking through the White House, looking for the cloakroom because we had to go, and the Secret Service come through—'People, step to the side, the president's coming through'—and President

Bush comes walking through the hallway, looks at me and says, 'I'll see you down there, dude!' [laughs] And in that moment I thought, 'I want to drink whiskey with this guy! I want to sit at a bar with this motherfucker!!' It's just hard to imagine these people as people. But they are."

Grohl had long been familiar with this dichotomy, between stardom and the reality of the people behind the facade. He'd spent over two decades when his very presence could stun fans to sputtering silence, and yet he wore his stardom more lightly than most, and was always trying to disarm the nerves of those he met. Because, when it comes down to it, he knew he was just a human being, not some kind of a god.

"To this day, when I think of Nirvana, it doesn't seem that different to me to Scream, or Dain Bramage, or Freakbaby or any of the other bands I was in as a kid," Grohl told me in 2005. "Some of them might have gotten platinum albums, some of them might have worked at a furniture warehouse on the weekend, but they're just bands, just people. Do I imagine the Pope is an angel sent from heaven? No, he's just a human being. Do I imagine

Above: Singer, songwriter, drummer, guitarist, producer, filmmaker, interviewer—is there anything Dave Grohl can't do?

Jimmy Page spawned from a jackal in Egypt? No, he's just a great guy, a human being, and he got to play music. It's hard for me to think of things in terms of cultural relevance, because I don't have that perspective on it. It's hard to be that objective, when you were *in* the band. Honestly, it was just a band.

"Admittedly," he added, laughing, "It's hard for me to accept that Led Zeppelin were 'just a band.' But I can say it about Nirvana." And, doubtless, about the Foo Fighters, too. Just bands, perhaps. But *what* bands.

Sonic Highways

Released: November 10, 2014
Label: Roswell/RCA
Recorded: September, 2013 July, 2014
Electrical Audio, Chicago
Inner Ear Studios, Arlington County, Virginia
Southern Ground Studios, Nashville, Tennessee
Studio 6A, Austin, Texas
Rancho De La Luna, Joshua Tree, California
Preservation Hall, New Orleans
Robert Lang Studios, Seattle
The Magic Shop, New York City

PERSONNEL:
Dave Grohl: lead and backing vocals; rhythm guitar; acoustic guitar, cymbals, and EBow on "Subterranean;" production
Pat Smear: rhythm guitar, lead guitar, producer
Nate Mendel: bass guitar, producer
Taylor Hawkins: drums, backing vocals, producer
Chris Shiflett: lead guitar; "devil Pickin'" on "Congregation"; backing vocals on "In The Clear"; producer

Additional personnel:
Mark Braud: trumpet on "In The Clear"
Zac Brown: Devil Pickin and backing vocals on "Congregation"
Gary Clark Jr.: lead guitar on "What Did I Do?/God As My Witness"
Charlie Gabriel: clarinet on "In The Clear"
Ben Gibbard: backing vocals on "Subterranean"
Chris Goss: backing vocals on "Outside"
Drew Hester: percussion on "Congregation," tambourine on "What Did I Do?/God As My Witness" and "I Am A River"
Ben Jaffe: tuba on "In The Clear"
Rami Jaffee: clavinet; organ; Mellotron; piano; Wurlitzer electric piano; backing vocals on "In The Clear," Space Keys on "I Am A River"
Ronell Johnson: tuba and backing vocals on "In The Clear"
Barrett Jones: EBow on "Subterranean"
Freddie Lonzo: trombone on "In The Clear"
Los Angeles Youth Orchestra: strings on "I Am A River"
Clint Maedgen: saxophone and backing vocals on "In The Clear"
Rick Nielsen: baritone guitar on "Something From Nothing"
Jim Rota: backing vocals on "In The Clear"
Peter Stahl: backing vocals on "The Feast And The Famine"
Skeeter Thompson: backing vocals on "The Feast And The Famine"
Tony Visconti: string arrangement on "I Am A River"
Joe Walsh: lead guitar on "Outside"
Kristeen Young: backing vocals on "I Am A River"
Butch Vig: producer

TRACK LISTING:
All tracks written by Dave Grohl, Taylor Hawkins, Nate Mendel, Chris Shiflett, and Pat Smear except where noted

1. "Something From Nothing" (featuring Rick Nielsen) Electrical Audio
2. "The Feast And The Famine" (featuring Peter Stahl and Skeeter Thompson) Inner Ear Studios
3. "Congregation" (featuring Zac Brown) Southern Ground Studios
4. "What Did I Do?/God as My Witness" (featuring Gary Clark Jr.) Studio 6A
5. "Outside" (featuring Joe Walsh) Rancho De La Luna
6. "In The Clear" (featuring the Preservation Hall Jazz Band) Preservation Hall
7. "Subterranean" (featuring Ben Gibbard) Robert Lang Studios
8. "I Am A River" (featuring Tony Visconti and Kristeen Young) The Magic Shop

The 38th BRIT Awards, The O2, London, UK, February 21, 2018

The Sky Is A Neighborhood

"I've never done anything for twenty years. When I worked at Shakey's Pizza, I didn't think I'd be there for twenty years. When we started the Foo Fighters, I didn't think we'd be here for twenty years."

DAVE GROHL

"The fourth of July next year marks the twentieth anniversary of the first Foo Fighters record coming out," said Dave Grohl, towards the end of our 2014 interview, his toothy, wide-mouthed grin swelling even more toothy and wide-mouthed with pride. "So we're playing the stadium where I grew up and went to see shows as a kid." His eyes lit up as he described the celebration he had sketched out. "It's crazy: it's Foo Fighters, Buddy Guy, LL Cool J, Troublefunk, Heart…A bunch of different guests. And I'm leading a motorcycle rally into the stadium, with fireworks and the whole deal. [laughs] I mean, how many twenty-year anniversaries do you get?"

It was a great plan. One of the best plans laid by men or, indeed, mice. And it unraveled in a flash, three weeks before the show, after Grohl tumbled offstage and broke his leg while performing with Foo Fighters in Gothenburg, Sweden. The break was nasty enough that the Foos' imminent set headlining the UK's Glastonbury Festival was instantly canceled (Florence and the Machine took their place), and a further four European shows had to be postponed, including a two-night return to Wembley Stadium.

"It was a beautiful night, a beautiful stadium, 52,000 screaming people—Dream gig!" a remorseful Grohl wrote in an open letter posted four days after the Gothenburg mash-up. "Two songs into our set, I made a mad dash to the right of the stage during 'Monkey Wrench' to shred some tasty licks for the kids up front. Well—wait for it—I definitely shredded something. (ZING!) Wound up dropping about twelve feet, dislocating my ankle and snapping my fibula like an old pair of take-out chopsticks. Not good. I told the audience I'd get fixed up and come right back to finish the show ASAP. Shock? Probably. But, I couldn't stand the thought of such a perfect night going to waste!"

Paramedics bundled the prone Grohl onto a stretcher, cutting opening his trousers and popping his ankle back into place. "I asked if I could get back onstage to finish the show," Grohl wrote, "but they said I needed a cast (which was twenty minutes away at the hospital) to hold my ankle in place. So I looked my EMT [emergency medical technician] Johan in the eyes and said 'Well, then you're coming up there with me right now and holding it in place until they can bring the cast here. Ready?' He stared at me wide-eyed for a second and said, 'OK, let's go…' All in all, it was without a doubt the single most bizarre Foo Fighters show in the entire twenty years of being a band."

After the show, x-rays revealed the full extent of the damage Grohl's tumble had wrought. Immediate surgery was required, which left Grohl with six metal screws in his leg, and a warning from his doctors to "lay low for a while." This involved canceling the shows, to Grohl's evident regret, but, as he wrote, "I need to make sure we have YEARS of gigs ahead of us…" But he couldn't bring himself to cancel the twentieth-anniversary show, especially with all his special guests already booked.

And so it was that, on July 4, 2015, Dave Grohl rode into the Robert F. Kennedy Memorial Stadium in Washington, D.C. not on a Harley Davidson, but in the lap of a throne he designed himself, while in the hospital blitzed on Oxycodone. And the throne looked a lot like something Dave Grohl might design while stoned off his gourd on high-grade painkillers, his back resting upon a roundel containing a ceremonial Foo Fighters logo, rimmed with spotlights and sprouting guitar necks out of every orifice, like H.R. Giger meets the Guitar Center. It was from here that Grohl conducted proceedings, his right ankle encased in plaster and kept suspended, but never impairing his ability to rock.

Support came from a rogues' gallery of guests from the *Sonic Highways* show, a diverse bill including LL Cool J, Joan Jett and her Blackhearts, Buddy Guy, Heart, and Troy "Trombone Shorty" Andrews. But it was the main attraction that shone brightest that night, for an epic set that drew more heavily from the track listing of that debut album than any Foos show in years, while revisiting the highlights from their entire career. It was a set list so swaggeringly confident it could open with "Everlong" and go on from there without fear of having peaked, a barnstorming twenty-two-song set that also found time to cover, if only briefly, Van Halen's "I'm The One," Queen's "Another One Bites The Dust," Yes's "Owner Of A Lonely Heart," and Queen and David Bowie's "Under Pressure." Taylor had his moment to shine too on "Cold Day In The Sun," before closing out with fireworks soundtracked by Hendrix's rendition of "The Star Spangled Banner" and AC/DC's "You Shook Me All Night Long." A night unashamed to look uncool having this much fun.

The event might have overwhelmed a lesser frontman, but Dave Grohl took it in his one-leg-in-plaster-ed stride. He'd long ago learned not to fear the wide open spaces stellar rock stardom opened up for him. That night he was no longer some drummer who had been thrust to the microphone, but a rock superstar in his own right, one who'd lived, lost, and loved, and recorded it all in the grooves of eight albums—one a double—with more

Opposite: The leg injury Grohl sustained while performing in Gothenburg scuppered the Foo Fighters' 2015 tour plans, but didn't stop him finishing the show from a wheelchair.

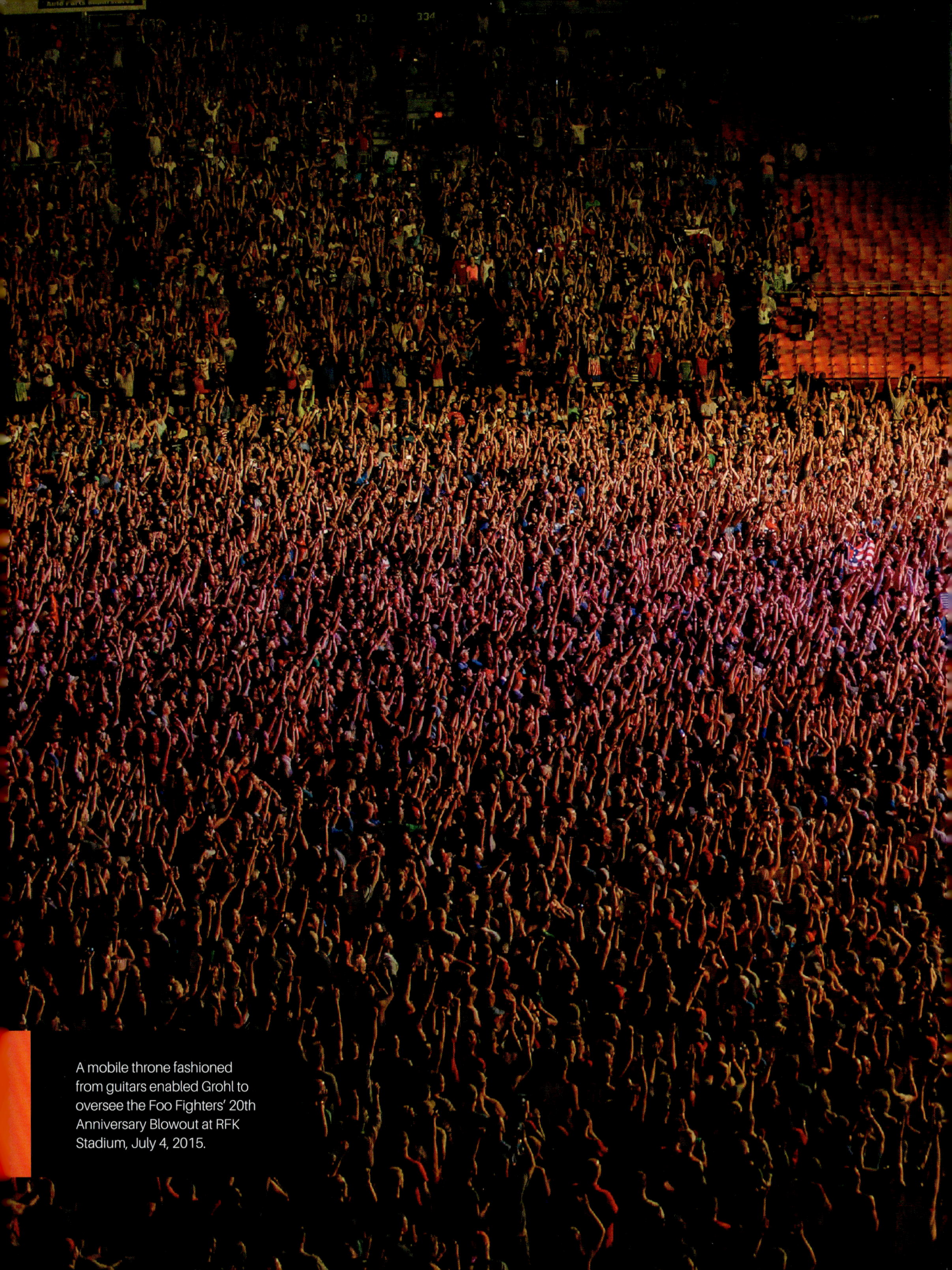

A mobile throne fashioned from guitars enabled Grohl to oversee the Foo Fighters' 20th Anniversary Blowout at RFK Stadium, July 4, 2015.

The Sky Is A Neighborhood

Left: A closer look at Grohl's throne; he'd later lend it to a similarly incapacitated Axl Rose for the Guns N' Roses reunion tour.

Below: Grohl invited a slew of guests to the Foos' 20th Anniversary Blowout, including Pete Murano and Trombone Shorty.

doubtless to come. A rock superstar who'd shepherded his Foo Fighters through outrageous fortune and misfortune, who'd lost friends along the way but made scores more, who no longer had to say "Fuck it" to get through the night, whose faith in his music had been proved time and time again and was now unshakable. A rock superstar who moved and talked onstage with the same supernatural ease he did off of it; to generations of fans the nicest man in show business, the best friend they'd not met yet, who placed his faith that night in those who shared the stage with him, and the thousands in the audience ready to sing along with every note. A rock superstar who knew that everyone there that night would love nothing more than to meet his mother, the saintly Virginia Grohl, so he could show them where he came from. A rock superstar celebrating twenty years of this band he fashioned from old friends and kindred spirits, twenty years since that album he'd blasted through in a week, that was now recognized as a rock 'n' roll classic.

"I've never done *anything* for twenty years," Grohl marveled from the stage. "When I worked at Shakey's Pizza, I didn't think I'd be there for twenty years. When we started the Foo Fighters, I didn't think we'd be here for twenty years. But I'm glad, on our twentieth anniversary, that we're here tonight, with you guys." Grohl began strumming the unmistakable, jazzy chords of "For All The Cows," Pat and Nate and Chris shadowing his notes, Taylor licking gently away at his hi-hat and snare. "I remember when I recorded this song, I played it for my mother," Grohl continued, before looking to the wings. "Ms Virginia Grohl. Come out! Come on mom, get out here!" The diminutive Virginia walked out to her son, out to his throne, and gave him a kiss on the lips. "The first time I played this song for my

> "The first time I played this song for my mom, she said, 'It sounds like Richard Marx' ... You know you're doing something right, if you write a song your momma likes..."
>
> **DAVE GROHL**

mom, she said, 'It sounds like Richard Marx,'" he grinned, as the crowd erupted into laughter. "Now, I don't know how many of y'all went to Fairfax High School, went to Annadale High School, went to Thomas Jefferson High School...How many high schools did you teach at, mom? My mother taught high school, public school, for thirty-five years. She's the most amazing woman in the world, so let's hear it for Ms Virginia Grohl, because we wouldn't be here if it wasn't for her! You know you're doing something right, if you write a song your momma likes..."

That night, as fireworks exploded in the sky to the sounds of sainted rock 'n' roll, Dave Grohl must have looked to the heavens and asked himself how long it would last, and where this ride would take him next. He'd long since ascended to the rock 'n' roll constellation, a man who could rub shoulders with Beatles, share the microphone with Lemmy. He must've known, even as modest as he was, that he belonged up there, with the stars. The sky was no longer the limit. The sky was now his neighborhood.

Opposite: Dave's mum, Virginia, has been his constant supporter, and was the guest of honor at his 20th Anniversary Blowout. She's even written a book about Dave.

Left: Blues legend Buddy Guy, who'd proven such a valuable interviewee on *Sonic Highways*, lent his best licks to the 20th Anniversary Blowout.

The thing with anniversaries is that they bring with them what Spinal Tap's David St. Hubbins perceptively described as "too much fuckin' perspective." Twenty years since the first Foo Fighters album also meant twenty-one years since Kurt Cobain had committed suicide, twenty-two years since the release of Nirvana's remarkable, tortured, molten *In Utero*. I'd interviewed Dave around the time of that album's twentieth-anniversary re-release, and he admitted the process of listening to and approving the new remasters had been no walk in the park.

"Of all of the Nirvana recordings, *In Utero* is the most difficult for me to listen to, not only because it was our last album before everything ended, but because just the sound of it reminds me of that difficult time," he told me. "Because it was a difficult time. Anyone who listens to that record can tell. . .It's not a Christmas album. The legacy of *In Utero* is of a band being true to themselves. Had we gone out and made an overproduced pop album to try and sell another thirty million records, it would have been a lie. And so, *In Utero* is entirely real. But would I sit down with a glass of wine and listen to that album at home? No I would not. It would fuckin' break my heart."

For all Dave's abundant popularity and success, there were inevitably detractors in rock fandom and the music press, for whom Dave's post-Nirvana career was somehow a betrayal of the purity and nihilism of *In Utero*, a betrayal of a Kurt Cobain they never knew and yet felt they did. Kurt would never have jammed with Queen, they whispered. Kurt would never have played soft-rock power ballads like "Learn To Fly," never have "played the game" like Dave had, probably never have sat opposite an American president to discuss the redemptive power of American music.

But there were no more chapters in the Nirvana story after *In Utero*. There should have been. There should have been albums'

> "Of all of the Nirvana recordings, *In Utero* is the most difficult for me to listen to, not only because it was our last album before everything ended, but because just the sound of it reminds me of that difficult time. But would I sit down with a glass of wine and listen to that album at home? No I would not. It would fuckin' break my heart."
>
> **DAVE GROHL**

worth of new Kurt Cobain music, or he should have quit and gone on to find joy in family life and obscurity somehow, to search more for that elusive peace and happiness. The Kurt Cobain story ended in 1994, and god, how everyone wished it hadn't. But there would be more chapters in the Dave Grohl story, more Dave Grohl music. He wasn't about to burn out or fade away—that one element of the supposed romance of rock and especially punk rock had thankfully eluded him. And more fool you if you hadn't listened closely enough to the passion with which he delivered "Walk's" refrain, howling with the same intensity and veracity with which Kurt had communicated his angst and agony, "I'm on my knees, I never wanna die, I'm dancing on my grave, I'm running through the fire." He was a lifer. And life was to be lived.

He was a bandleader. He was a floating drummer in the wildest pirate ship in rock 'n' roll, and key member of endless further side-projects and collaborations. He was an esteemed documentary film-maker, founder of one of LA's finer studios, owner of a fuckin' Neve desk, goddammit. He was a husband and a father. And the lust with which he lived every one of those roles was invested in Foo Fighters' best music, and that's what Foo Fighters' fans could sense, what they identified with, what spoke to them. Foo Fighters' music was about life, was the music of their lives. Their own lives were invested now in those songs, forever.

"Fifteen years ago I had open-heart surgery," the comedian and perhaps the greatest of the late-night talk show hosts David Letterman said to his audience, on the night of his final episode of the *Late Show*, May 20, 2015. "I was off the show for five or six weeks, and Sheila Rogers [Letterman's producer] said, 'On your first show back, is there anything special you would like, musically?' And I said, 'Well, yeah, what about Foo Fighters?' They'd been on four or five times. She said, 'Well, I'll ask them. But it could be a problem.' 'Well, just ask them. Also, there's a song I would like to hear, it's special to me, it's been meaningful through my heart recovery; it would be just great.' Two days later, she calls back and says, 'They're on tour in South America . . .But they canceled the tour! They're coming back to do the show, and they'll do the song you asked for.' Happily, since then, we've been joined at the hip. God bless you, gentlemen. . ."

Foo Fighters played that song, "Everlong," for Letterman again that night, behind footage and images of the most memorable moments in Letterman's thirty-five years as a talk show host, its emotive peaks and tangled valleys and valedictory crescendos ringing louder and more powerfully than ever. Foo Fighters had become America's rock band, their music the soundtracks to people's lives. With that intimacy, that cosiness, that familiarity came a transaction: it obscured just how restlessly experimental they were, Grohl on a quixotic mission to never make the same album twice, to put himself in unfamiliar and creatively challenging positions, making music with friends and strangers, and always changing up the equation.

Their next album would be their most experimental yet. Twenty years and counting into their journey, Foo Fighters were going. . .pop?

The truth would, of course, prove more complex, but yes, the ninth Foo Fighters studio album would be graced by guest appearances from Justin Timberlake and Boyz II Men's Shawn Stockman, with production by Greg Kurstin, whose works have

Right: Producer Greg Kurstin, pictured here with his The Bird and the Bee bandmate Inara George, was a crucial influence upon *Concrete and Gold*.

sold over sixty million copies worldwide, including "Hello" by Adele, while his past clients include Pink, Sia, Lily Allen, and Kylie Minogue. In 2017 alone—the year he worked with Foo Fighters—Kurstin brought home four Grammy Awards, including Song of the Year, Album of the Year, Record of the Year, and Producer of the Year. If, in 2017, you wanted to make an album that sounded like the "state of the art" (not to mention the "state of the product that shifted the most units"), Greg Kurstin was the guy you tapped up.

Not that Dave Grohl had much interest in making another Foo Fighters album at first. Indeed, in March 2016, rumors abounded that the Foos were being put on ice and that Grohl had an eye to pursuing a solo career—ludicrously, because Grohl had performed The Beatles' "Blackbird" solo at that year's Oscars ceremony. Taylor had given an interview in January confirming that the group were going on "indefinite 'ihateus'"—his term for "hiatus"—and stating that, "we did so much the last five or six years. . .the world needs a break from us for a little while."

But when the Oscars performance stoked the Grohl-goes-solo whispers to ear-splitting volume, the group released a YouTube video—preceded by dramatic build-up on Twitter, suggesting a "big announcement" was coming—lampooning the hysteria surrounding the band's future. "Maybe it's time to do my own thing?" Grohl told a deadpan Butch Vig, before footage of Dave exploring a risible electronica career, while his bandmates scrabbled to find a new singer (Nick Lachey, formerly of boy band 98 Degrees, guest-starred as an auditionee, singing an impressive take of "Everlong.")

"For the millionth time, we're not breaking up," ran the message at the end of the video. "And nobody's going fucking solo!"

Foo Fighters: The Band That Dave Made

Left: Performing with Zac Brown on the *Late Show with David Letterman*. Letterman is a huge fan of Foo Fighters.

However, Grohl's enthusiasm for music was tested as 2015 wore on. The realities of his recuperation bit hard, and after the high of the July 4 extravaganza at the Kennedy Center, two to three hours of heavy physical therapy every day—a course that would last for almost a year—left him feeling bleak and not wanting to even touch his guitar. He told the other Foos that the band would go dark for another 365 days, at least. This signified the longest lay-off the Foos had ever endured. "It got," he told *Rolling Stone* magazine, "a little dark."

But as the Mamas and Papas sang, the darkest hour is just before dawn. And halfway through Grohl's self-enforced break from music, he picked up his guitar and penned a new song. It was a song rooted in darkness—a reaction, perhaps, to 2016's presidential election, and the malign forces unleashed by the rise of Donald Trump—but one with a classically Grohl-ian message of uplift, beckoning the listener to "wake up" and to "run for your life with me."

"Run," the lead single from *Concrete and Gold*, released in June 2017 but played live by the Foo Fighters since February of that year, opened with lush, soft guitars but soon snapped awake with perhaps the heaviest, most gnarly punk rock riffage of the band's career, and Grohl's most fevered howls. The single spoke to the sprawl of sounds the new album would encompass: the polyphonic spree of Grohl's influences and interests, painted on his vastest canvas yet.

To make sense of these jarring elements, Grohl sought Kurstin's assistance. "I just imagined the sound moving outwards," Grohl told *Music Week*. "Just, sonically, to push it 'out.' Greg is a fucking genius. He's a brilliant producer, and he had this sonic intuition that I have never seen in anybody else."

Working with Kurstin involved a total change of modus operandi for the Foos, who'd recorded their last albums in Dave's garage (*Wasting Light*) and all over America, with a documentary crew in tow (*Sonic Highways*). His initial plan had been to record the new album onstage, before an audience of twenty thousand, as a live album, but Grohl felt that PJ Harvey's 2016 album *The Hope Six Demolition Project*—the production of which she presented as an art installation at London's Somerset House, inviting the public to watch while she worked—had beaten him to this particular plan. Instead, Grohl took the album in the opposite direction. "I thought,

'What's the strangest thing for the band to do at this point?'" he told *Rolling Stone*. "And then I realized it was just to go into a studio and make a fucking album like a normal band."

Grohl had first fallen for Kurstin's unique approach to music after he heard his band The Bird and the Bee, a duo featuring Kurstin and singer Inara George, whose four full-length releases to date included an album of Hall & Oates cover versions. When Kurstin met Grohl and the Foo explained his concept for the next album, Kurstin said, "It was like he was describing a heavy metal *Sgt. Pepper* odyssey." Grohl, meanwhile, hankered after "the album I have always wanted to make, because of the love of seventies AM gold radio, and the love of a band like Motörhead."

The album was recorded at Hollywood's EastWest Studios, and it was the constant slew of high-profile artists also recording at EastWest that afforded Grohl the chance to work with Timberlake and Stockman. But while Kurstin pushed the Foos' paradigm further than it had ever gone before, experimenting with new drum and guitar sounds in the studio, and opening up new options for the group, the resulting album was everything Foo Fighters had been so far, but amplified, and cranked to eleven. The riffs could be savage, they might even take out your eye—but the tracks were also slathered in creamy harmonies and wreathed around irresistible melody. It was, without a doubt, Grohl's most explicitly Beatles-influenced album yet. Earlier in his career, critics had dismissed him as the grunge Ringo; *Concrete and Gold*, however, proved Grohl was the grunge McCartney, a master melodicist who could also rock like a beast, and was deftly but profoundly experimental, without making too much of a big deal about it. (McCartney, meanwhile, played The Beatles' Dave Grohl on *Concrete and Gold*, guesting on drums for Hawkins's "Sunday Rain.")

Concrete and Gold was an album with depths, its songs sophisticated, both musically and lyrically, an album where opener "T-Shirt" could see Grohl whisper "I don't wanna be queen, just keep my T-shirt clean," before mighty Queen harmonies hammered in, where sonic triumphalism could slam headlong into bleak lyrics like "If there's one thing I've learned, If it gets much better, it's going to get worse." Musically, the album dipped deep into the past—"The Sky Is A Neighborhood" made like *Abbey Road* was a metal album, "La Dee Da" had a sense of vastness like *Physical Graffiti*-era Zeppelin, and the closer "Concrete and Gold" glided like a comfortably numb Pink Floyd. But these songs were also viscerally connected with the world of 2017, where progressive dreams had collided headlong with fake populist realities, where unrepentant pussy grabbers held the highest office and Nazis were running down protesters in the street.

It was here that Grohl's eternal optimism began to shake. "I'm a father now, I have to consider more than I used to," he told *Kerrang!*, "and I think I've realized we're not all as free as we were before. It became clear there was so much more threatening all of our lives than I'd considered before. I have three daughters who are going to survive me for decades—how are they going to get on unless there's some positive and progressive change?" Grohl contributed towards effecting that change the ways he could: with his money, with his words, and with his music. "I just wanna sing a love song, pretend there's nothing wrong," he sang, on "T-Shirt." But he knew something *was* wrong, and that disquiet proved the undertow of this epic, triumphant album.

The *Concrete and Gold* tour kicked off at Laugardalur Park in Reykjavik, Iceland on June 16, 2017, and would stay on the road, in manageable bites scheduled around the band members' family lives, until October of the next year, traversing Europe, America, South America, and Asia. The tour marked Rami Jaffee's inauguration as a full Foo Fighters member, not just touring keyboard player. And now they were six.

But Grohl's next project saw him finally "go solo," as the panicked rumors had dreaded he might. Between the roomy gaps of the Foos' touring schedule, Grohl got a hankering to cut a piece of music entirely on his own—a twenty-two-minute instrumental piece, on which he would play every single instrument. If that wasn't challenge enough, he'd film a video of the performances, so it could be used to publicize the Join the Band Music Lessons Studio, an operation dedicated to teaching kids to play music.

"To any musician, young or old, a roomful of instruments is like a playground," Grohl explained, in the video. "I'm like a kid in a candy store." And at that, the black-and-white video portrayed seven separate Dave Grohls walking into a recording studio and, through the use of canny video techniques, playing the instrumental "Play" as an ensemble. The track was a reminder of the mighty, morphin' quality to Grohl's music, an ever-shifting piece that swung between irrepressibly muso flourishes and passages of dreamy, trippy introspection and colossal, towering blasts of heavy, metallic, psychedelic riffology, the multiple Grohls playing in perfect simpatico with each other. It was also undeniably inspiring stuff, offering a hand to the viewer and saying, "If you only learned how to play a musical instrument, you could enjoy a moment like this yourself." As if to prove that point, within a fortnight of the video hitting

Opposite: *Concrete and Gold* witnessed keyboardist Rami Jaffee officially join the Foo Fighters as a permanent member, after twelve years as a sideman.

Fueling rumors of going solo, Grohl performs live at the 88th Oscars® in 2016.

Opposite: Headlining Glastonbury's Pyramid Stage, 2017. The kind of gargantuan rock experience Grohl and cohorts take in their stride nowadays.

YouTube and going viral, one fan, Leander Widmoser, had already uploaded a video of himself playing along with the track, managing to hold tight on the song's every twist and turn.

Grohl really hadn't made things easy for himself while making the video. "It was really just to see if I could pull it off," he said on the late-night talk show *Jimmy Kimmel Live!* "To see if I could do these full takes without making mistakes and actually memorize that much music. I thought it would be like a really freaky mushroom trip if I film it and make it look like there's seven of me in the room together. And so I came up with the idea, and thought, well, that's kind of stupid. And then someone said, 'Well, we booked the studio, we've got the camera guy, it's all set up.' And I thought, 'Well, now I've got to write the music.' So I wrote this big long thing, but as I was doing it, I couldn't help but think about my kids, who are musicians, and watching them challenge themselves and really try to push themselves and learn new stuff. So I'm inspired by watching these kids and their friends, they have bands and they're really trying. And you never lose that as a musician. It's like a lifelong obsession, just pushing yourself to get to the next level."

In any other musician's mouth, such words would feel like fake homilies. But for Dave Grohl, it was the truth. Two decades into Foo Fighters' career, over three decades since he'd snuck into the ranks of Scream, music still possessed that rejuvenating, redemptive hold over Grohl. Early in his career, he'd witnessed his friend Kurt's Icarus-like journey through stardom, a trip that left him at odds with the music he loved, at war with his audience, and, ultimately, dead by his own hand at the age of twenty-seven. Grohl was, unquestionably, better equipped to deal with success than his former bandmate, who'd been stricken with depression, still reeling from a miserable childhood, and under the influence of a debilitating heroin addiction that skewed his outlook and left him drowning in shame and helplessness. But surviving success with his ego intact, making the Foo Fighters a healthier environment than his previous band, prizing his family above everything, and figuring out how to manage the business of show without damaging his love for the art and heart of music, these were all conscious decisions for Dave Grohl.

"You have to remember, the period of time between Nirvana getting popular and Kurt dying was really just a couple of years," Grohl told me, in 2014. "So it was all condensed in that short period of time, and it was really intense...Unless you're emotionally designed to withstand something like that, it can be really traumatic. And we were kids—I was twenty-two. I look at younger musicians going through the same thing, cross your fingers and think, god, I hope they're okay, that they get a break. With the Foo Fighters, it was a much more gradual incline—we went from playing the Astoria in London [capacity: 2,000] to playing Milton Keynes Bowl [65,000] over a good eighteen years. So every step of the way you grow a little bit, you get a little stronger, a little more resilient and a little more set in your ways.

"It took us a little while to work out how to say 'No.' We used to do everything, and then after a while we realized, self-preservation kicks in and I decided, 'Okay, I don't want to do everything, and I don't want to burn it out, let's make it last by doing it slowly.' Like when we did those two gigs at Wembley, that was, like, the pinnacle of our success. And when you're standing onstage like that, you just remember the demo tapes that started the whole thing rolling. And that night, I was like, we gotta go home. I don't want to get used to this yet, before this becomes 'just a gig.'"

Twenty-three years in, jadedness is still an alien concept on Planet Foo. And if Dave Grohl has any say in it, it always will be.

> "I'm inspired by watching these kids and their friends, they have bands and they're really trying. And you never lose that as a musician. It's like a lifelong obsession, just pushing yourself to get to the next level."
>
> **DAVE GROHL**

"We used to do everything, and then after a while we realized, self-preservation kicks in and I decided, 'Okay, I don't want to do everything, and I don't want to burn it out, let's make it last by doing it slowly.' And when you're standing onstage like that, you just remember the demo tapes that started the whole thing rolling. I don't want to get used to this yet, before this becomes 'just a gig.'"

DAVE GROHL

Concrete and Gold

NME Album of the Year, 2017

Released: September 15, 2017
Label: RCA/Roswell
Recorded: December, 2016-May, 2017
EastWest Studios, Hollywood, California

PERSONNEL:
Dave Grohl: lead vocals, guitars
Chris Shiflett: lead guitar, backing vocals
Pat Smear: rhythm guitar
Nate Mendel: bass
Taylor Hawkins: drums, percussion, backing vocals, lead vocals on "Sunday Rain"
Rami Jaffee: keyboards

Additional personnel:
Justin Timberlake: backing vocals on "Make It Right"
Shawn Stockman: vocals on "Concrete And Gold"
Inara George: vocals on "Dirty Water"
Alison Mosshart: vocals on "La Dee Da" and "The Sky Is A Neighborhood"
Dave Koz: saxophone on "La Dee Da"
Paul McCartney: drums on "Sunday Rain"
Taylor Greenwood: backing vocals on "T-Shirt"
Greg Sierpowski: Optigan on "Happy Ever After (Zero Hour)"
Kinga Bacik: cello on "The Sky Is A Neighborhood"
Thomas Lea: viola on "The Sky Is A Neighborhood"
Ginny Luke: violin on "The Sky Is A Neighborhood"
Jessy Greene: violin on "Happy Ever After (Zero Hour)" and "The Line," cello on "Concrete And Gold"
Greg Kurstin: synth bass and vibraphone on "The Line," production

TRACK LISTING:
All tracks written by Dave Grohl, Taylor Hawkins, Nate Mendel, Chris Shiflett, Pat Smear and Rami Jaffee except where noted

1. "T-Shirt"
2. "Run"
3. "Make It Right"
4. "The Sky Is A Neighborhood"
5. "La Dee Da"
6. "Dirty Water"
7. "Arrows"
8. "Happy Ever After (Zero Hour)"
9. "Sunday Rain"
10. "The Line"
11. "Concrete And Gold"

Above: Though born from tragedy, joy has been the common theme of the Foo Fighters' twenty-five years as a unit. Long may they all prosper...

Picture Credits

B: Bottom, **L**: Left, **R**: Right, **T**: Top
Alamy: **COVER**: Guy Bell **10R**: Iconographic Archive **12, 71**: Everett Collection, Inc. **14, 15, 36-7**: Pictorial Press Ltd **17R**: Records **18-9R** Phil Rees **24, 131**: CBW **25**: David Noton Photography **57, 92**: TheCoverVersion **110-1R**: Amanda Rose **148-9, 194, 204**: WENN Rights Ltd **196**: Gonzales Photo **P218-9**: PictureLux/The Hollywood Archive **222-3L**: ZUMA Press, Inc. **BACK COVER**: Roberto Finizio/Alamy Live News **Getty Images**: **1, 16-7, 54-5, 64, 186-7T, 209R**: Kevin Mazur/WireImage **13, 216**: Jim Steinfeldt/Michael Ochs Archives **20-1, 43, 48-9, 60-1, 70, 76-7, 90-1, 140-1**: Jeff Kravitz/FilmMagic **7, 26-7, 30, 44-5, 88-9, 94-5, 96, 105**: Mick Hutson/Redferns **9**: David Corio/Redferns **11**: Mark and Colleen Hayward **22-3, 28**: Michel Linssen/Redferns **29, 45R, 65** Ebet Roberts/Redferns **31**: Catherine McGann **33, 34-5, 38-9, 112**: Gie Knaeps **46-7**: Gary Leonard/Corbis **51, 52-3**: Tim Mosenfelder **58-9, 66-7, 74-5, 80**: Martyn Goodacre **68-9, 120-1R**: Kevin Cummins **78L**: Kurt Krieger **78-9R**: Margaret Norton/NBC/NBCU Photo Bank **83**: Brenda Chase Online USA, Inc. **85**: Michael Ochs Archives **86**: DMI/The LIFE Picture Collection **97**: SGranitz/WireImage **98, 102-3, 211**: Theo Wargo/WireImage **99, 109**: Sebastian Artz **100-1**: Hayley Madden/Redferns **110L, 126**: Scott Gries/ImageDirect **114-5**: Frank Micelotta **116-7T**: Fin Costello/Redferns **118**: Annamaria DiSanto/WireImage **122**: Ron Galella/WireImage **127**: Kevin Winter **130, 134-5, 168-9**: Martin Philbey/Redferns **138L**: Tabatha Fireman/Redferns **138-9R, 144-5**: Louise Wilson **142**: Richard Corkery/NY Daily News Archive **146T**: Fairfax Media **152-3**: Getty Images **154B**: MJ Kim/MPL Communications Ltd/MPL Communications Ltd **160-1**: Tracy Leeds/NBC/NBCU Photo Bank **162-3L** Rick Smee/Redferns **164-5L**: Rich Polk/Getty Images for Stagecoach **165R**: Mark Venema **171**: Ray Tamarra **172L**: Steven Dewall/Redferns **172-3R**: Lisa Haun/Michael Ochs Archives **176-7**: Scott Melcer/WireImage **180-1**: Mike Pont/FilmMagic **184-5** Jason Squires **187B**: Michael Buckner **190-1L**: Taylor Hill/FilmMagic **191R**: Brian Cassella/Chicago Tribune/TNS **192**: Tony Woolliscroft/WireImage **193**: Gary Miller **195**: Jay West/WireImage **197**: Rick Diamond **198-9B**: Cliff Lipson/CBS **199T**: Chris McKay/WireImage **206-7, 208-9L**: Kyle Gustafson/The Washington Post **213**: Allen Berezovsky **214-5**: Jeffrey R. Staab/CBS **Rex Shutterstock**: **2-3**: Nitu Mistry **4, 156**: Richard Young **18**: Phil Rees **40**: Ian Dickson **62**: Hayley Madden **84**: Granger **106**: REX/Shutterstock **124-5, 150T**: Kevork Djansezian/AP **129**: John D Shearer/BEI **132-3**: Sipa **136-7**: Tracey Nearmy/EPA **143**: Most Wanted **146-7B**: Jesse Wild/Future Publishing **150-1B**: Action Press **154-5T**: The Fa **158-9**: Amanda Schwab/Starpix **166**: Startraks **174-5, 188-9**: John Shearer/Invision/AP **178-9**: Canadian Press **182-3**: Chris Pizzello/AP **200**: Matt Sayles/AP **202-3, 220**: James Gourley **210**: Nick Wass/Invision/AP

ALBUM COVERS: **10** *Bleach* Tracy Marander, Charles Peterson photography, Lisa Orth cover design **15**: *Nevermind* Robert Fisher artwork, art direction and cover design, Kirk Weddle cover photography **17**: *In Utero* Robert Fisher art direction, design, photography, Alex Grey illustrations **24**: *2112* Hugh Syme graphics, Yosh Inouye photography **37**: *Foo Fighters* Jaq Chartier jacket artwork, Tim Gabor art direction, album design, Jennifer Youngblood cover photography **50**: *"Ring Spiel" tour '95* Nanette Roeland cover art, Jeff Schulz design **73**: *The Colour and the Shape* Jeffery Fey, Foo Fighters, Tommy Steele art direction, Jeffery Fey, George Mimnaugh design, Andy Engel, logo design, Josh Kessler, photography **84**: *Frampton Comes Alive!* Ian Dickson, Richard Aaron photography, Stan Evenson design **92**: *Live Killers* Queen/EMI Records **93**: *There Is Nothing Left to Lose* Henry Marquez, Foo Fighters art direction, Danny Clinch photography **101**: *Songs for the Deaf* Hutch artwork **113**: *One by One* Rupesh Pattni graphic design, Anton Corbijn photography, Joshua White photography, illustrations, Raymond Pettibon artwork, illustrations **116**: *Kill 'Em All* Harold Risch, Sheri Risch design, graphics, layout, Gary Lee Heard back cover photography, cover photography **120**: *Probot* Stephen O'Malley design, Michel "Away" Langevin, cover art **131**: *Led Zeppelin III* Zacron cover artwork **135**: *In Your Honor* Dan Winters photography, Danny Clinch photography, Brett Kilroe, Robin C. Hendrickson additional art and "Crest" concept, Kevin Reagan art direction, design, Bret Healey design **157**: *Echoes, Silence, Patience & Grace* Don Clark art direction, design Laura Kleinhenz, Ben Watts photography **163**: *Red Light Fever* Morning Breath Inc. art direction and design, Wiley Hodgden, Laura Kleinhenz photography **167**: *Chris Shiflett & The Dead Peasants* Jack Butler cover photography, Simon McLouglin art direction, design, Jeff Nicholas art direction, design, photography **170**: *Foo Fighters Greatest Hits* Morning Breath Inc. art direction and design **177**: *Wasting Light* Morning Breath Inc. art direction and design, Steve Gullick photography **201**: *Sonic Highways* Morning Breath, Inc. art direction and design, Stephan Martiniere cover illustration, Ringo photographs, Andrew Stuart photographs, **223**: *Concrete and Gold* Andy Carne art direction, artwork, design